Congratulations
Graduation from Northwestern.
Dick V—
6/22/2002

Enough Money!

June 21-22, 2002

For our beloved daughter, Rachel, on the occasion of your graduation from Northwestern University. May you always have enough of all that makes you happiest —
—Mom & Dad

Enough Money!

—Nobody has it—
—Everybody has it—

How to Create and Manage
Financial Success in Your Life

by

Richard E. Vodra, CFP

Published by

>   Richard E. Vodra
>
>   6827 Montivideo Sq. Ct.
>
>   Falls Church, VA 22043

Copyright© 2000, 2001 by Richard Vodra. All rights reserved.

Library of Congress Number: 2001118161
ISBN #:   Hardcover   1-4010-2472-6
          Softcover   1-4010-2471-8

All rights reserved. No part of this book may be reproduced or transmitted in any form or by any means, electronic or mechanical, including photocopying, recording, or by any information storage and retrieval system, without permission in writing from the copyright owner.

Second edition, October 2001.

The 700% Solution and Lifetime Balance Sheet are registered trademarks of Richard E. Vodra

This publication is designed to provide accurate and authoritative information in regard to the subject matter covered. It is sold with the understanding that the author and publisher are not engaged through this book in rendering specific financial, legal, accounting or other professional services. If expert assistance is required, the services of a professional should be sought.

Every effort has been made to make this book as complete and accurate as possible within the structure of the topics covered. However, there may be mistakes, either typographical or in content. Further, tax laws and other realities are subject to change and revision. Therefore, this book should be used only as a general guide. The author and publisher specifically disclaim any liability or loss that is incurred as a consequence of the use and application, directly or indirectly, of any information presented in this book.

If you do not wish to be bound by the above, you may return this book to the publisher for a full refund.

This book was printed in the United States of America.

To order additional copies of this book, contact:
Xlibris Corporation
1-888-7-XLIBRIS
www.Xlibris.com
Orders@Xlibris.com

Contents

Forward—Why this book, and why now 9

Introduction: What "Enough Money" means to you
    Seeing through the financial snow 15
    How to use this book 16
    Simple rules work 17

The Lifetime Balance Sheet®—your guide to financial
    independence 19

The Seven Rules of Prosperous Living
    —all at once 33
    —in a little more detail 35

How to take care of your financial life
    Managing your cash flow 45
    Your income and your Career Development Fund 57
    Prepare for retirement with The 700% Solution® 67
    Save money for college costs 88
    Manage risk with insurance 92
    Estate plans for you and your family 106
    Give money away and stay prosperous 118
    Use help when it gets complicated 125
    How to invest what the rules produce 134

Your One Page Financial Plan and Your Seven Promises ... 150

Appendix
　　Creating an Investment Policy Statement 163

DEDICATION

This book is dedicated to my children, Paul and Katie, to Roberta, and to all the wisdom and love found in the members of the Nazrudin Project.

FINALLY, A MONEY BOOK THAT WORKS!

There is a tremendous need for a simple, short, comprehensive book about money, comparable to "The One Minute Manager," "Life's Little Instruction Book," and "Don't Sweat the Small Stuff." A book about the forest, not the trees. At the same time, the book must be believable, with an attitude that isn't patronizing, with goals and rules that are attainable, and supporting a range of value systems and lifestyles.

Personal finance is a great frustration for many, many of us. We know we have to take care of it, but money appears complicated and intimidating. We look for advice, and find too much–books that are hundreds of pages long covering dozens of topics, a shelf full of magazines that change every month and seem to provide both too much and not enough. We get the message that you have to be an expert even to start out. That approach is wrong-headed and dangerous.

Americans, as the Introduction points out, are faced today with an increasing responsibility for managing their own future and an incredible (and distracting) range of choices to get the job done. In an era of more stability and fewer tools, maybe it was easier. Today, it's hard. A lot of people are in immediate trouble, and many more are creating future problems by acting without awareness of how all their major decisions fit together. They want a simple, short guidebook.

The time is right for this book. We've entered a period of "growing up" about money. At a national level, we've balanced the national budget, and even begun to talk about Social Security. At a global level, the problems from Wall Street to Asia remind us that boom times and easy credit catch up on the players, often leaving a bad hangover. At a personal level, the early Baby Boomers can start to see what they have to do if they ever want to retire. The press attention to that problem—whatever the leading edge of Boomers is doing gets press attention—will inspire younger people to pay more attention to money issues earlier in their lives.

When you want to learn what to do, you want to start with something small and comprehensive that helps you succeed. *ENOUGH MONEY!* is that book.

ACKNOWLEDGMENTS

A book like this emerges from the lessons learned from hundreds of clients, colleagues, teachers, and friends. What I think of as my perspective on financial planning grew from their experiences and wisdom passed to me, which I molded but did not entirely create afresh.

The actual writing of a book is both personal and communal. The encouragement, ideas, reactions, and corrections from many people kept me going, and kept me on what I hope is the right path. At the risk of omitting some who helped me, I would like to thank Tom Barrett, Tracy Beckes, Bev Chapman, Hank Dunn, Jim Gottfurcht, Deb Johnson, Tracy Kellum, George Kinder, Roberta Lee-Driscoll, Diane Lobasso, Cicily Maton, Olivia Mellon, Diane Miller, Colleen Mohyde, Aileen Nowatzki, Bruce Pickle, John Rains, Laura Schoenbrun, Ari Tuckman, Margaret Vanderhye, Anne Volo, Bob Veres, Katie Vodra, Paul Vodra, William Vodra, Terry Walsh, Roron Wisniewski, and Marcee Yager. Each of them made contributions to the book you now have, and I am grateful to them all.

INTRODUCTION

Imagine yourself in a room full of people. The speaker asks:

"How many of you have enough money to do the things you want to do?"

No hands go up.

"What if I could double the amount of money you have. Would that be enough?

One or two hands.

"What if I could triple your money—your income and your investments. Would you be able to do all you want with that?

Most people smile and say yes.

"Do you know someone with three times as much money as you have? Would they raise their hand?"

Oops. Maybe not.

Let's try another approach. "Imagine that you suddenly have a change in your life. Your parents or your children need help, and it's going to require 10 to 20% of your income for as long as you can see. Or your job has been reorganized, and you've lost a big chunk of your income. Or you've made a commitment to give away 10% of your income every year. If you had to, do you think you could adjust your life so you could pay for all your real essentials, even with less money than you have now?"

Nearly everybody admits that they could.

We've just demonstrated the two uncomfortable facts about money:

> Nobody has enough money.

> Everybody has enough money.

* * * * * *

Why do I think this book can help you, when I don't even know who you are? Because you (like all of us) live in an economic society that puts you in a very difficult place. More than ever before in history, your financial present and future depend on decisions and actions you have to make, and the scope of those decisions seems to grow every year. Changing the way you approach your money can have a profound effect on your life. When you see the big picture, your path will be both clearer and more manageable. The rules you *need* to know to guide your financial life can fit on a business card. There's a lot you *can* know and a lot that *might be useful* to know, but there's not a lot you *need* to know.

This book invites you, challenges you, and enables you to take care of your own financial life.

—Making this decision is your surest path to lifetime prosperity.

—Nobody else is going to take the responsibility and do this for you.
—The rules are easy enough to understand, so you *can* succeed.

SEEING THROUGH THE FINANCIAL SNOW

The list of financial choices facing people is overwhelming, and getting worse. Not too long ago, if you wanted a *mortgage*, you took out a thirty-year fixed rate loan. Today mortgage brokers have dozens of "programs" available, allowing you to decide how much cash to put into the loan, how long the initial rate should be fixed, and if it changes, how often, what the index should be that changes are based on, and so on. Under the current tax laws, there are more than a dozen different "flavors" of *Individual Retirement Accounts*, each unique in some way: how money can be added, the tax treatment of contributions, the tax treatment of withdrawals, or the rate money has to be taken out. In the 1980's, there were already more *mutual funds* than there were stocks on the New York Stock Exchange—now there are well over 10,000 such funds.

If you think about *retirement*, not only do you have to decide how much to contribute to your savings plan at work—and that plan may be a 401K plan, or a 403B plan, or a SIMPLE IRA, or a Thrift Savings Plan, or something else—but you have to allocate your additions among as many as several dozen investment options. Even *paying for groceries* requires you to decide between using cash, a check, a debit card, or one of the half-dozen credit cards most Americans carry.

When it comes time to think about the other end of your life, you are confronted by more decisions: *life insurance* (How much? Whole life? Variable life? Universal life? Variable universal life? Term? Five-year term? 10-year? Minimum premium? Maximum funding? Who should own the policy?) and *estate plans* (Gifts?

Revocable trusts? Irrevocable trusts? Who gets how much?). Young couples have to decide how to arrange their finances; older people have to decide what to do with their retirement distributions. Even if you understand all the options, it isn't easy to make good decisions about your own money, balancing values, emotions, and objective facts.

With this level of complexity, it's no wonder that most financial self-help books have hundreds of pages. It's also no wonder that most people still struggle, despite (or because of) those books. The bad news is that hardly anybody can get it *all* precisely right. The good news is that it isn't hard for you to do *all the important things* well enough and move on with what really matters: your family, your health, your career, your community, your spiritual life, your friends.

HOW TO USE THIS BOOK

ENOUGH MONEY presents everything you need to know about money, in about 150 pages. You'll be treated with respect—no "idiots" or "dummies" here. The essentials of money are not complex, and you can learn and live them.

The core idea is the Lifetime Balance Sheet, and the core practices are the Seven Rules for Prosperous Living that flow from the Lifetime Balance Sheet. The Lifetime Balance Sheet helps you answer the questions of how you are doing and what you can afford, by putting all your resources and obligations in a single picture. Your financial life gets better as you learn how to expand your resources and measure your obligations, which is what the Seven Rules are all about.

You'll see the Seven Rules all at once. (That's the part that fits on a business card.) You'll read a little about each rule, then a chapter on each rule. Finally, you'll see how to fit them back together in your life, and get started creating successful financial habits with Enough Money.

SIMPLE RULES WORK

The idea that the long version of the "rulebook" may be too much for average people to master isn't new, or limited to money questions. The "food police"–nutritional experts–are constantly trying to figure out and teach us what we "need to know" about eating well. We hear about vitamins and phytochemicals and monosaturated fats and insoluble fiber, and we don't want to put the effort into understanding. Then one major food store, working with the National Cancer Institute, came up with "Strive for Five": try to eat at least five servings of fruits and vegetables each day. If you can do that, most of the other problems will take care of themselves–your fat intake will go down, your fiber will go up, and so on. It's not perfect or precise, but you can understand it. It even builds in a little leeway: you can "strive" for the goal, and not be condemned if you don't make it every day.

Consider another analogy, that of spirituality, and think of someone trying to grasp the essence of Christianity or Judaism. They might try to understand the religion by reading the sacred texts. They will dive into Genesis and give up soon after, wondering what anyone could find exciting and meaningful in there. The Bible is a very long and not-too-accessible book. One translation has 1547 pages in the Old Testament and 451 pages in the New Testament. That's almost 2000 pages of stories and lessons and rules, even before consulting the libraries of commentaries that those pages have generated in both the Jewish and Christian traditions.

Other people enter from a different door. They may have a profound experience that prompts a commitment and a decision to learn more. They will find the words of Jesus or the Prophets, or experience some of the love and mystery, and then rediscover the Ten Commandments, and finally, perhaps, want to read the whole story. When these people finally turn to Genesis, it is with a motivation and an understanding that provides meaning that the other readers miss.

So for matters as prosaic as eating or as profound as the purpose of life, the rules aren't complicated. They may not be easy or convenient to follow, but we're better off as we try.

Think about some other choices. The decision to become physically fit must precede effective learning about the mechanics of exercise, and the decision to eat well precedes expertise on nutrition. All the lectures, gym classes, and other encouragement are less effective than a personal choice to become stronger and healthier. Then you join the gym, start walking, and pay attention. The decision to be financially responsible precedes useful learning about the nature of mutual funds and variable rate loans. When you decide to deal with your money, then you are ready to learn how.

But in that tender time when your faith or your energy is shaky, you don't need debates about religion or dissertations on the relative values of nutritional supplements. You need simplicity, honesty, encouragement, and forgiveness, and a reminder of how the pieces fit together to support your goal.

The rules about money haven't been whittled down to one or two yet, but seven are enough to support a life of financial independence and responsibility illustrated in the Lifetime Balance Sheet. As you follow along, you'll learn how to have a more peaceful and satisfying financial life.

THE LIFETIME BALANCE SHEET®

Your guide to financial independence

This book started with a true story that illustrates two contradictory facts about personal finance:

Nobody has enough money.
Everybody has enough money.

If you can afford to buy this book and have the motivation, you have enough money to do all the things you have to do, but not enough to do everything you might want to do. There are people in our society, maybe 20% of the population, who may in fact be so poor or so rich that these truths do not apply to them, but most of us live in that zone where this is reality.

So what is it you want?

Charles Dickens' creation Oliver Twist, answering for most of us, simply said, "More." But that's an endless path to frustration. Only 400 people or families appear in the Forbes Magazine annual list of the 400 wealthiest Americans, and 399 of those know they aren't at the head of the line.

How about what we hope money can buy? Power? Love? Security? The truth is, of course, that money can help with these sometimes, but not ultimately provide them. Mother Theresa had a kind of power that most of the Forbes 400 could only dream of, despite her vow of poverty. We all know of millionaires who live and die alone. We know of tycoons whose companies or marriages or families fail.

Money is best thought of as the tool to pay our bills and satisfy some of our obligations. The wise use of money, in the getting and spending of it, allows us to live as grown ups. It's not the most important thing we need–we also need to spend time with those we love, and live a life with integrity, and pursue worthwhile goals–but how we deal with money is a measure of the quality of our lives.

Do you want to be financially independent? Most people do. In fact, that's the number one goal listed when people seek advice. Do you believe you can achieve it? You can.

There are two kinds of financial independence. The first is having resources that produce enough income to allow you not to work for a living any more. This is valuable, and we'll talk about it when we discuss retirement planning.

Real financial independence, though, is the ability to use your income and resources to meet all your financial obligations, now and in the future. Independence isn't the freedom to ignore everyone; it's the freedom that comes when you act responsibly.

Real financial independence is what most people want. They don't have it, often, because they don't understand how to make it happen and what's involved. Since few of us have somebody to bail us out of trouble, the irony is that we have lives that turn out to have been financially independent. Those lives often aren't very satisfying, though, and we don't do the things we want, and there can be a lot of stress.

One big reason that motivated people have trouble handling

their money is that they can't see the big picture. You know about how much money you'll make this year, and you can get a good idea of how much money you have and owe right now. Accountants have invented tools for those things: an income-expense statement (called a profit-and-loss statement for a business) and a balance sheet. But neither works well enough to help you manage your money over the long term. (You may not realize that you prepare most of an income statement every year. The IRS calls it a Form 1040.)

Want to try a better way? Let's call it a **Lifetime Balance Sheet.**

The only time you've probably prepared a regular balance sheet is when you either applied for a loan or filled out a government disclosure form. You listed everything you *owned* (investments, home, etc.) on the left side, under Assets, and put everything you *owed* (mortgages, credit cards, etc.) on the right side, under Liabilities. Your Net Worth is the excess (you hope) of your assets over your liabilities.

A regular balance sheet is pretty limited as a planning tool, because it leaves out a lot of important information. It leaves out most of what you're going to have during your life, and most of what you really are going to owe. What you need is a better idea of how much money you're going to have to work with throughout your life, and what you're going to do with it.

That's why you should think in terms of Resources, not just about Assets. You need to expand from a list of your Liabilities, to think about all your Obligations. If the Resources side is bigger than the Obligations side, you will be OK. If it isn't, you'll need to make changes.

Your biggest Resource is probably your ability to work for a living. If you expect to earn a decent income for the next ten, twenty, thirty, or more years, the value of all of the income you will earn is greater than whatever financial assets you've accumulated so far (or, if you're older, at least it compares in size). Another big Resource is money you are going to receive as a retirement pension or other benefit. You may have a good expectation of inheriting money someday (though relying on that can be risky.).

When you list your Liabilities, most people put down their mortgage, any credit card balances, and maybe a car loan. Good start, but again, you're leaving out many important Obligations.

The first one most people add is education for their children, and that should include all the other special costs of raising sons and daughters, from diapers to soccer teams to braces.

The next cost is the "regular" cost of Daily Living Forever for yourself (and your spouse, if you're married). This includes the years while you are working, and the cost of living in retirement—food, clothing, utilities, vacations, health care, cable TV, and all the other items in your budget that you'll be buying for the rest of your life.

There are special costs, too, that some people include. You may expect to have to pay for care for your parents someday. You may want to leave money to your children when you die. You may want to make a substantial charitable gift during you life or at your death. You may want to buy a vacation home.

The Lifetime Balance Sheet simply collects all the Resources you anticipate, and that's what you have available for all the Obligations you have. When you see it all at once, you can start to plan realistically.

To use the Lifetime Balance Sheet for planning, turn the process on its head. What you ultimately want to know is what you can afford to do with the money you will have. You want to know how to balance what you want for today with what you'll want for the future. You want to know how you can increase your income and resources so you can do more. Today and tomorrow, income and expenses—all these interact, but until now it has been hard to see how everything fits together.

The following pages explain in some more detail how the

Lifetime Balance Sheet works. If you don't want to spend time on this process now, the important points to remember are that your income and expense decisions have long-term effects, you ultimately can't spend more than you'll have, and all these decisions are related to each other. Some people will want to try this out for themselves, while others want to get on with the book. If you're in the second group, you can just skim through the next few pages.

How can you put all this—what you own, what you'll make, and what you'll spend—on one piece of paper? There's a critical concept that makes it possible, a tool that compresses many years of money into a single number. "Present value" is the name financial planners give for this key idea, and like most things, it is simple once you get it.

Suppose someone offered you a choice between receiving $100 every year for ten years, or $250 today. Which is a better deal? Most people should take the $100 per year, assuming they were confident they were actually going to get all the payments. It's not very likely that anyone could invest $250 so well that you could count on getting $100 per year for ten years. But what about $900 today as the alternative to $100 per year? Where's the break-even point? What is $100 per year for 10 years really worth?

Another way of asking this is, what is the *present value* of $100 per year for ten years. If the interest rate is 5%, the answer is about $772. You can invest $772 at 5% and pay yourself $100 for ten years before the money runs out. In other words, if you were offered a choice of $772 or $100 per year when interest rates are at 5%, in theory it should not matter which you took.

If you could make more than 5%, you would earn more money on your investment, so the lump sum (present value) needed to produce the stream of $100 checks is smaller. With 8% interest, the present value of $100 a year for ten years is only $671, not $772.

That covers money you get or pay every year. How much would you be willing to invest today to get $1000 back all at once ten years from now? At a 5% interest rate, the present value of that is $614. Why is this important? It's one way you know, for example, whether you have saved enough for a child's college costs.

Let's apply this idea to your planning, and your Lifetime Balance Sheet. Your biggest Obligation is likely to be the costs of daily living. After paying taxes and your mortgage, suppose you spend $2000 per month (or $24,000 per year) on other living expenses, and you expect to spend at that rate for twenty more years, ignoring inflation for a minute. How much of an obligation does that represent in today's money, if we use a 5% (after tax) interest rate? The answer is about $305,000. Another way to say that is that if you invested $305,000 at 5%, you could spend $2000 per month for twenty years before you ran out of money.

When you prepare your Lifetime Balance Sheet, then, you will have an Obligation of $305,000 for this part of your cost of living. For each item in your life, we will similarly estimate an amount that you will need to have. For your mortgage, and other obvious debts, we will use the actual amount you owe.

Turning to the Resources column, if your take-home pay is $5000 per month after taxes, and you plan to work for 20 more years, the present value of your income is $760,000.

These examples have used a 5% interest rate, because that has been common for saving accounts and low-risk investments recently. However, that figure doesn't factor in taxes and inflation, and you can't ignore those. Taxes take about 25% of your income, and inflation has been running about 1.5% to 2% per year recently. When these are included, *it's more likely that your real rate of return, after taxes, inflation, and fees, will be 2% or less. Therefore, we will use 2% in figuring present value numbers.*

Let's return to your income. You should get raises in the future to at least keep up with inflation, so $5000 per month for 20 years is actually worth about $980,000 in today's money, using the 2% factor. If you could spend $10,000 on an educational program that would increase your income by $500 per month for 20 years, the payoff would be worth $100,000 to you—a very good investment.

In principle, every stream of income, whether starting now (like a salary) or a pension (starting when you retire) can be converted to a present value amount. By the same principle, every dollar you're going to spend in the future can be expressed in today's money.

The Lifetime Balance Sheet totals up the value of all the Resources and Obligations you can identify, all expressed in today's money.

Right now, to help you see this in action, here's a Lifetime Balance Sheet for the fictional Mike and Karen Jackson. Mike and Karen both work, they have two children and a house and retirement plans. They're 40, and their grandparents are still alive, so the Jacksons expect to be around a long time. Follow along, referring to the accompanying charts.

There are also instructions in italics with each point to help you create your own worksheet on the following page.

LIFETIME BALANCE SHEET

Mike and Karen Jackson

RESOURCES

SAVINGS & INVESTMENTS		
You Control	Investments	$75,000
Others Control	Retirement Plans	$80,000
NON FINANCIAL ASSETS	Home	$0
	Other Property	$0
FUTURE EARNINGS	$120,000 - 20 years	$1,800,000
FUTURE BENEFITS	Social Security	$100,000
SPECIAL RECEIPTS	Inheritance	$100,000
TOTAL		**$2,155,000**

OBLIGATIONS

PAST CONSUMPTION	Credit Cards	$3,000
CURRENT USE DEBT	Mortgage	$200,000
	Car Loan	$10,000
INVESTMENT DEBT		$0
SPECIAL NEEDS	Education	$80,000
	Raising Children	$109,000
	Care for Parents	$75,000
	Charity, bequests	$0
SUBTOTAL		$477,000
BALANCE AVAILABLE		$1,678,000
	Daily Living Forever	
	Other Goals	

LIFETIME BALANCE SHEET
Your Worksheet   Date: _____

RESOURCES

SAVINGS & INVESTMENTS		
You Control	Cash	$
	Investment accounts	$
	Custody accounts	$
Others Control	Retirement Plans	$
NON FINANCIAL ASSETS	Home	$
	Other Property, cars	$
FUTURE EARNINGS	Income x yrs x 75%	$
FUTURE BENEFITS	Social Security	$
	Pensions	$
SPECIAL RECEIPTS	Inheritance	$
TOTAL		$

OBLIGATIONS

PAST CONSUMPTION	Credit Cards	$
	Student Loans	$
CURRENT USE DEBT	Mortgage	$
	Car Loan	$
	Other long-term debt	$
INVESTMENT DEBT	Margin Loan	$
SPECIAL NEEDS	Education	$
	Raising Children	$
	Care for Parents	$
	Charity, bequests	$
SUBTOTAL		$
BALANCE AVAILABLE		$
	Daily Living Forever	$
	Other Goals	$

Start with "Savings and Investments." Here, we use familiar real numbers. The Jacksons have $75,000 in investments in their names ("You control"). *Add up what you have in cash (and money market accounts), in investment accounts (including IRAs), and in custody accounts for your children.* They have another $80,000 in employer retirement plan accounts ("Others control"). *Add up what you have in 401K, profit-sharing, or other retirement plans held with your employer.*

Under "Non-Financial," they own a house worth $275,000, and cars and other property worth $60,000, for a total of $335,000. However, since they don't intend to sell the cars or move to a smaller house, these aren't assets they plan to use to support their standard of living, so no value is recorded. *Only include a value here if you plan to move to a less expensive house someday, or will sell your art collection to fund your retirement.*

In a traditional balance sheet, we'd have finished with their assets, for a total of $490,000. In the Lifetime Balance Sheet, we don't include the house and cars, but we keep going.

Under "Future Earnings," the Jacksons earn a combined $120,000, including their employers' match on their 401K plans, and they expect that to grow for 20 years at 2% faster than inflation. (Taxes take about 25% of your income on average, so reduce all income numbers by 25% to get after-tax figures.) The value of their after-tax income is $1.8 million (!), computed by multiplying their income times the years remaining times the after-tax percent, 75%. *Estimate the value of your income by multiplying your income (including regular bonuses) times 75% times the future years you plan to work.* "Future Benefits" include pensions (which they may not receive) and Social Security (which they still plan on). As a very rough estimate, the lump-sum value of future Social Security benefits for most people is about $140,000 in today's money. *Use a $140,000 value for Social Security, add one year's income if you have pension benefits you have already earned. If you are already receiving a pension (such as from the military), multiply your pension times the years you expect to live times 75%.*

"Special Receipts" includes money you expect to receive in inheritances, gifts, trust funds, alimony, or other payments. The Jacksons are confident their parents and grandparents on one side should leave them at least $100,000. They may get more, but aren't willing to count on it. *Only Include amounts you can count on; it's usually better not to include anything.*

These items bring the Jacksons' total Resources up to $2,155,000, in today's money. Because of future inflation, they will actually have more than $3 million pass through their hands, maybe much more, but that's so uncertain that it should be ignored for now. They feel much better. Instant millionaires! *Add up your numbers, and feel good for a minute or two.*

Obligations need to be added up next. "Past consumption" refers to credit cards and general debts for past spending. The Jacksons have $3,000 in this category. *Add up any ongoing credit card balances, and any student loan balances.* "Current Use Debt" refers to debts used to buy the non-financial assets they are still using. They have a mortgage of $200,000 and car loans totaling $10,000. *Include your mortgage, your car loan, and any other installment debt or home equity loan.* (If they had investment debt—if they had borrowed to buy stock, for instance—it would be in another category here, as a "real" liability.) *Include any money you have borrowed against your investment accounts or your retirement plans.*

In a traditional balance sheet, we'd stop here. Remember that their assets came to $490,000. They have liabilities of $213,000, so their net worth is $277,000. *How much money do you owe other people? What's your net worth?*

But we're just beginning. Turn to "Special Needs." The Jacksons have two children to educate. They are willing to pay the entire cost of four years for each at the state university (costing $10,000 per year today). In today's money, that comes to $40,000 each, or $80,000 total. *Multiply the number of children you have times the years they will be attending college times the cost today of a college they might attend times the* share *you plan to pay. If your children attend private elementary or high school, do the same calculation.* They estimate that the extra costs of raising children come to $1000 per month for ten years, or $109,000. *Extra costs of $500 to $1000 per month per child are reasonable. Multiply by the number of months until age 18, then subtract 10% to get the present value estimate.*

They may have to support a parent in a nursing home someday, and want to set aside $75,000 for that purpose. (Think of that as a "negative inheritance.") *If you think you'll support other family members, include an estimate of the cost here.* "Charity and Bequests" are gifts that you are so sure you will want to make, you include them as obligations. The Jacksons don't want to include anything here for now. *If you have a large special gift planned, here is where it goes.* Their "Special Needs," the money to be spent on children and others, total $264,000 in today's money.

So far, the Jacksons have identified $477,000 in obligations for paying their mortgage and other debts, raising their children, and supporting their parents. They have about $1,678,000 left for other goals, including their Daily Living Forever for 50 years.

To determine how much you can spend, use this table, which shows how much spending can be sustained for various periods with $1,000,000. The Jacksons have $1.6 million and plan to live 50 years, so they multiply $32,000 (per million at age 40) times 1.6 (millions), getting $51,200, which they should round to $50,000.

Your age	Years to go	Spend per million
30	60	$29,000
40	50	$32,000
50	40	$36,000
60	30	$45,000

If they want their spending to track their income, they can live on about $50,000 now (plus $17,000 in mortgage payments and $12,000 for costs for their children, or a total of $79,000), and still save for retirement, pay their taxes, and save for educating their children. But if they spend all they have available today—say, $90,000 after taxes—they won't have enough for the things they want to do later on. Some of that $90,000 needs to be saved. As their income rises, their spending can grow, too.

Suppose the Jacksons want to buy a vacation property for $150,000, and expect that they will spend $1000 per month keeping it up, getting there to use it, and on activities there. The real cost of that house is not $150,000, but is actually (over 20 years) $200,000 for using it plus $150,000 for buying it, or $350,000. This is a 20% of the $1.6 million they were planning to use for living expenses. Buying the house could create long-term problems if they don't adjust elsewhere.

Two things about the Lifetime Balance Sheet are especially attractive. The first is that it violates many basic principles of accounting. Accountants really like precision, and there isn't much here. Accountants don't like to confuse income statements with balance sheets. This actually combines them. Instead of a snapshot of the present, the Lifetime Balance Sheet compresses today and the future onto a single estimate.

The other important thing is that the concept matters much more than the numbers. Fill out your worksheet to see the shape of your Lifetime Balance Sheet and get a sense of how you are doing. But the Lifetime Balance Sheet deals with the future, and the future can't be predicted with accuracy. Once you figure out that Obligations cannot be bigger than Resources, you've got the Big Idea. Once you realize that "real" retirement is only possible when you can ignore any future earnings and still have enough Resources, you understand why you must invest for the future.

The Rules that follow in this book all flow from the Lifetime Balance Sheet idea. If you can stop spending money on interest payments, you can redirect that money toward other Obligations. The most controllable way to increase your Resources is to improve your employment income, which you can do though your Career Development Fund. You can calculate how big your retirement Obligation is, and create investment Resources to meet it. You can think about insurance as a way to create Resources when earnings disappear before Obligations do.

You can use your Lifetime Balance Sheet to decide if you want to reduce Obligations or increase Resources as the best way to achieve Financial Independence. And you can rest with the knowledge that you understand your overall picture: where you are, where you're going, and how you're going to get there.

You have the power to create and maintain prosperity for yourself and your family by following seven easy-to-understand rules. Read them once, then read about them in the chapters that follow. Then you'll have a chance to put it all back together and have your financial life on the right path.

THE SEVEN RULES OF PROSPEROUS LIVING

1. Take care of your current cash flow. Keep your housing and car costs reasonable, and pay off your credit cards every month. Get the balances to zero, and keep them there.

2. Take care of your income by reinvesting 3-5% of your income into your career.

3. Take care of your retirement by saving and investing to reach The 700% Solution–assets equal to seven times your income.

3A–If you have children in school, put money aside for their college education.

4. Take care of the risks you face by owning good insurance on your life, your income, your medical care, and your property.

5. Take care of your family and others important to you by updating your estate documents at least every four years.

6. Take care of your community and your spirit by giving away more than 2% of your income every year.

7. Take care of your time and your sanity by asking for help when the money questions become complicated or overwhelming.

Non-rule: There is no rule on investing. How you invest your money matters, but not as much as following the Seven Rules does.

THE SEVEN RULES OF PROSPEROUS LIVING

IN A LITTLE MORE DETAIL

Rule 1: Take care of your current cash flow. Keep your housing and car costs reasonable, and pay off your credit cards every month. Get the balances to zero, and keep them there.

There are many aspects to managing your cash flow so that you move toward your goals, not away from them. The basic concept is to spend less than you make. For many Americans who don't do this, the trouble shows up most seriously in the use of credit cards.

Credit cards provide great convenience, but at a potentially great cost. They allow you to buy things quickly and without carrying a lot of cash around. You can swipe your card through a reader and buy gasoline or groceries, make phone calls, or buy a coat in a store you've never been in, possibly in a country and currency far from home. You get a consolidated bill which you can pay in full, without interest, by the end of next month. Pretty neat.

But if you fail to pay the bill in full, most cards take away any interest-free grace period and charge interest on every purchase from the first day. People who make only minimum payments on their cards often end up paying more in interest than they do for the items they bought—in other words, their cost of living doubles.

Many people carry a balance on their cards and keep it fairly level from month to month and year to year. Interestingly, this means that they're paying off their new purchases on a current basis. With discipline, if they could ever "clean up" their credit cards, they could keep them balance free, taking advantage of the convenience factor.

If you have a balance, give yourself some time to get out of debt. If your balance equals your monthly take-home pay, you can devote 10% of your pay to the old debt on the card and be debt free in a year or less. A balance of twice your take-home pay will take two years to pay off at 10% per month. At the end of that time, you'll be used to living within a new spending level, and you can put the 10% toward your own long-term goals. Crash dieting doesn't work any better with money than it does with weight.

Once you have a card with no balance, that should be the only card you use for new purchases, and it should be paid off in full every month.

Rule 2: Take care of your income by reinvesting 3-5% of your earnings into your career.

If you're working, your ability to earn a living is probably the most valuable asset you have. Certainly, from a financial standpoint, most people more than a few years from retirement expect to earn more money in the future than they have accumulated in savings and investments to that point. Of equal importance, what you do helps define who you are, your position in society, your self-image, and other aspects of your personality. (It's not the only thing, of course, but it is one of the central things.)

The job and responsibilities you have today, however, probably won't be your daily fare in five, ten, or twenty years.

The creation and destruction of entire lines of work seems to be accelerating, although it has been a feature of life for the entire history of America. If you define yourself by your current job, you are putting your identity and future under the control of employers and forces who not only don't care about you, they may not even know you exist.

Instead of thinking that you work for a company or other organization, realize that you work for "You, Inc." You, Inc., might be an engineering firm or a provider of human resource services with only one employee–you–that is currently "under contract" to whoever signs your paycheck. If that "contract" ends, You, Inc., still exists, and simply needs another contract.

A "real" business has to put aside some of its income, after paying all its bills and taxes, for marketing and research and development, so it will have products and customers next year, too. So do you, or more accurately, so does "You, Inc." You, Inc., needs to be sure that its employee has good skills, belongs to the right professional associations and goes to the right meetings, has some money set aside for finding new contracts (i.e., a job search), and so on. If You, Inc., does this consistently with 3-5% of its (your) income, and pays you the rest, you'll find that in a few years, your earnings are larger and more secure, and you are emotionally and professionally better equipped to handle the changes that will confront you.

Most people, experts predict, will have more than six jobs and three careers during their working years. Wouldn't it be nice to be in charge of that process?

Rule 3: Take care of your retirement by saving and investing to reach The 700% Solution–assets equal to seven times your income.

The number one financial planning goal for most people is retirement saving. We expect a long and relatively active life, which means we will either have to work forever or save money to pay our bills after we stop working. After school, we hope to work for 35 years (age 25 to 60) and live another 35 (to age 95). Obviously there must be a lot of savings during that period, if we're going to pull this off. But how much?

Most retirement calculators try to predict how many dollars you'll need decades in the future, using lots of dubious assumptions to generate a huge number that discourages almost everybody, and still doesn't tell you what you need to do today.

Everything about the future is unknowable, yet we have to take actions today to prepare for it. The 700% Solution gives a plausible answer and a course to follow now.

The details of The 700% Solution are presented later in this book. The bottom line is that you can retire reasonably after your late 50's if you have retirement assets equal to seven times your pre-retirement income.

To calculate what you need to do, all you need to know is your age, your income, and the amount you have saved for retirement so far. We assume your savings will grow a little faster than your income, and you can look up on the chart on page 84 to determine the rate at which you need to save from now on.

As an example, if you are age 40, making $80,000 per year, with $120,000 in various retirement accounts, you have 1.5 times your income set aside, which should grow to about 2.5 times your then-income by your age 65. To reach 700% by age 65, you need to save 14% of your income each year.

Remember that your savings includes the money your employer puts away for you, so if you have to save 14% and your company match is 5%, you only need to save 9%. Most people under fifty can save enough; if you can't (or don't), the alternatives are to work longer or live on less in retirement.

Rule 3A: If you have children in school, put money aside for their college education.

Planning for college varies between families more than most things. A good starting point is to assume that your total family obligation for four years of college will be about equal to one year's income. Keep the college funding decision in perspective. Parents shouldn't deplete all their assets without requiring sharing of the costs by their students.

Rule 4: Take care of the risks you face by owning good insurance on your life, your income, your medical care, and your property. Most financial planning is based on the hopeful assumption that we will have long, healthy, safe, and productive lives. More than ever before in history, the chances are pretty good you will. Yet we know that our lives and those of our friends and families are still full of uncertainties, and some of those events can produce financial disasters.

The basic rule is to buy insurance for those events that are not unlikely, where the financial impact is something you cannot handle yourself, and where the cost of insurance is not unreasonable.

Life insurance (which is actually death insurance, but they can't sell it that way) is used to fulfill financial obligations that remain after your death. The amount you need depends on what those obligations are (do you have children? does your spouse depend on your income?) and what other resources you have. Your insurance should last at least as long as the obligations do.

There are two ways to insure your income. Protecting against job loss we took care of in Rule 2. You protect yourself against the inability to work with disability insurance. Your current earnings limit the amount you can buy. Most people should own as much as they can.

Your medical care is insured through health insurance, which covers medical bills, and long-term care insurance, which covers nursing care where you live or in a nursing home.

Your property insurance covers your automobile and home, and the possibility that you'll injure other people. Review these frequently enough to be sure your property is adequately, but not overly, insured.

In property and medical insurance, a major part of the premium goes to administer the policy. Low deductibles (or short waiting periods) often result in very high premiums, so that unless you are very likely to have a claim, you will pay more than you get back. Remember the basic principle: only insure those losses you can't afford to pay yourself.

Rule 5: Take care of your family and others important to you by updating your estate documents at least every four years.
Estate planning is something that few people enjoy, and many people put off literally forever. Even (or especially) attorneys are notorious for ignoring this process. It is the process of making decisions now about your money in anticipation of the time when you won't be able to make them in the future. It once meant "writing a will," but it is now much more than that.

One important need for planning comes from the fact that many people will face a period of incapacity before they die, whether due to illness, dementia, a stroke, or some other factor. Without proper documents, created in advance, your family (if you have one at that point) will have to go to court and undertake the pain, publicity, expense, and inconvenience of a guardianship or conservatorship proceeding.

Further, the death rate is still one each. At some point the things you have now—money, property, and mementos—will be be passed on to others. Who should get what? When should they get it? Should there be any strings?

Do you have children? Unless you state your preference, your relatives can fight over who will be their guardians in the event of your death.

If everything you own, including the face value of your life insurance, exceeds $675,000 (an amount that is set to increase to $1 million in 2002, and grow more in later years), then the Federal Government may become one of your beneficiaries, unless you do some planning. The estate tax affects relatively few people, and it can often be eliminated or reduced with some simple techniques.

But even if you don't have a lot of money, planning is essential, and reviews are, too. Your resources change; your children are older; the couple you named as guardians for your children if something happened to you has gotten a divorce; you've moved; the laws have been revised. It's a good idea to have a good estate planning attorney—which is a specialty, so don't use a non-expert—review your documents on a regular basis. Pay attention to what's in them and update them as necessary.

Rule 6: Take care of your community and your spirit by giving away more than 2% of your income every year.

The other rules are about taking care of yourself and improving your cash flow and net worth. What's this doing here?

As we earn and accumulate money, we should ask ourselves what the money is for. Holding onto "our own" and only taking care of "ourselves" is a narrow and negative feeling. We are part of a community that exists beyond the legal structures we support with our taxes. Many of us have benefited directly from the generosity of others, and all of us are better off for having voluntary organizations in our local and national "neighborhoods." So from a practical, even selfish, sense, we should contribute our share of the cost of the youth programs, homeless shelters, churches, museums, wildlife preserves, clinics, and valuable parts of the world around us.

The benefits of giving can be more personal and less tangible. There is a joy and satisfaction in knowing that you helped change somebody's life. The gift can be direct (at a possible cost of a tax break, but don't let Congress steal your fun): pay for a child to go to camp, or send your children tickets for a vacation trip they can't afford.

There is another real benefit from giving money away. All of us would like to have more money than we have. We fantasize that if we only had a little bit more, we'd be OK. But when we make gifts, we're also telling ourselves deep down that we have enough, enough for ourselves and a little left over for others. We still might want more, but there's a peace that comes from generosity.

It is possible to be too generous, responding to every appeal from charity or children asking for help by giving more than you can afford. When giving cuts so far into your resources that health care, diet, and personal needs are threatened, it is time to make sure your priorities are in order. Say "no" when you need to.

Financial planning is about being able to sleep at night. Thoughtful giving can help.

Rule 7: Take care of your time and your sanity by asking for help when the money questions become complicated or overwhelming.

In the introduction of this book, and in every other financial self-help book and magazine, the complexity of financial life is made apparent. The number of decisions is large, the choices for each decision overwhelming, and the information mind-numbing.

If you enjoy getting into the details of money and want to handle everything yourself, recognize what you've committed to do. There are courses and books available to you to help you, for example, learn the nuances of mortgage financing for the one time every three to ten years you're going to use that knowledge. Understand, however, you could do yourself as much harm as good.

There are a few important principles—including the six other rules in this book—that should be followed for financial success. Find reliable people who will take the time to understand your goals and objectives, and who will teach you the impact of the decisions you make. (For example, in the real world, what's the difference between a one-year and a five-year adjustable rate mortgage?) Make your decisions about your goals, and listen to the advice of experts as to how to reach those goals.

The less you have to do, the more likely it is you'll make the decisions and move forward. If the specific choice doesn't really matter much, don't agonize over it.

A good choice for a general "expert" is a sensitive Certified Financial Planner practitioner, who should be able to be your financial coach. Call on estate planning attorneys, mortgage brokers, insurance professionals, accountants, and career counselors as needed. Don't let the fear of having your ignorance "exposed" keep you from dealing with your financial life. There is no shame in having enough of a life that you haven't spent lots of time learning the minutiae of financial mechanics.

The Non-Rule: How you invest your money matters, but not as much as following the Seven Rules does.
Many people think that financial planning is about, or mainly about, investing money. The Federal and state governments regulate planners through statues governing "registered investment advisors." Further, most people think investing money is about finding the "right" stock or mutual fund, and knowing what is going to happen in the "markets."

Many financial planners will tell you that more than 90% of the return you receive from your investments is based on the mix of assets you own (stocks, bonds, real estate, domestic, foreign, etc), and only 10% or less on the specific investments or when you bought them.

Wrong, and wrong.

Financial planning is about allocating your money between what you can spend today and what you have to set aside so you can have some to spend in the future. And the biggest determinant of your investment return is your behavior: not what stock or fund you buy or when you buy it, but whether you buy it at all, and whether you can leave it alone to grow instead of cashing it in for spending.

Nobody knows what the future will bring in terms of general or specific investments. Because we live in a capitalistic society that rewards the owners of profitable businesses, we expect that investments in businesses through buying stock will go up in value, but there will be years they won't.

If you think picking investments is fun or challenging, and your savings program is in place, there are lots of good books, magazines, and Internet web sites you can refer to. But if that describes you, you've probably already started. If investing is either threatening or boring to you, it's a good idea to return to Rule 7 and find an advisor to work with.

Suppose you resist hiring someone and want a basic guideline to follow. Recognize that everyone's different in how long they plan to invest, their ability to hold a course through bad times, and similar factors. You can make adjustments from the following plan: put half to two-thirds of your long-term money into a diversified group of stocks or stock mutual funds, a quarter to a third into bonds or bond funds, and 10-20% into money market funds. Another option is to buy two or three good balanced funds, and let the managers do the allocating. The exact investments you own matters, but not as much as getting started and keeping your commitment to paying for your future obligations while you can.

RULE ONE

TAKE CARE OF YOUR CURRENT CASH FLOW BY PAYING OFF YOUR CREDIT CARDS EVERY MONTH.

Credit cards, mortgages, car loans, and spending your income

Now you're ready to enter the next level of the book. You understand how your Lifetime Balance Sheet shows where your money comes from, and where it will go, both now and in the future. You've read the Seven Rules, and know all the basic things your money (and this book) has to cover. It's time to go through it again, to give you more perspective and ideas and help you make it work in your life.

With all the things you have to do to be responsible for your financial life, where do you start? With spending. And your appetite.

You'll have an income in the next twelve months. It might all come from one job, and you get paid every other Friday. You might get a pension and a paycheck. Your income might be "lumpy," from bonuses or commission income. Whatever it is, what are you going to do with it? (In Rule 2, we'll talk about how you might make your income bigger, but that's later.)

Most discussions about budgets and "spending plans" advise you to figure out where you are spending money today, and to divide it into fixed, variable, and discretionary categories. Then they tell you—or it feels like they tell you—to eliminate everything in the discretionary column, and save the money you used to spend. That works for a little while, but like most diets, not for long.

Since this book is talking about Enough Money for your lifetime, we need to challenge that framework. Nearly all your spending is probably fixed for the next month, while nearly all of it is variable and discretionary if you look ahead five or ten years. A few big choices can shape your financial success. The guidelines that follow will help you think about these choices.

To start out, pretend that your entire income for the next year is spread out on your dining table in Monopoly® money. (Some people find it fun and useful to do this exercise with actual Monopoly money.) Now start dividing it up into piles for the major categories of your financial life. Remember what you learned at the very beginning: you will not have enough money to do everything you *want* to do, but you do have enough for everything you *have* to do.

One pile is for income and Social Security taxes. It will be about 25% of your total income. Other piles pay for the other things you have to do: retirement, about 10%; career development, about 4%; insurance, another 4-5%; and education, about 4% per child per year. These will be discussed with the later rules. We will return to this allocation process in the concluding section of the book.

The money you have left can be spent on housing, cars, and everything else. By keeping the amount for housing and cars appropriate for your income, you'll have enough for everything else, too, including the credit cards. (More on them soon.)

WHY DO WE BORROW MONEY?

The theme of the Lifetime Balance Sheet, and of this Rule, is that when we're finished, all of us can only spend what we have. There is no "net" borrowing. Sooner or later, we have to pay what we owe. The more you can do that as you go along, the less money you spend on interest, and the more money you have for the things you want.

Some people pay cash for everything (except perhaps their house). They don't like debt, and avoid it diligently. Others finance many of their purchases, from their cars to their food, clothes, and other regular expenses. Often these debtors get into trouble because they can't pay back their loans. If you've ever worried about being in this second category—or if you are there now—these next pages are especially important for you. Even if you are now in control of your cash flow, it is good to understand the challenges involved in staying on top.

There are three basic reasons to borrow money. The first is to pay for something you'll use for a long time as you use it. If you plan to live in your house (either your current home or its replacements down the road) forever, it makes sense to pay the mortgage over many years. Similarly, a car that you'll drive for five years can be paid for (or saved for) over that same period.

The second time to borrow is when you think you'll make money on the money you borrow, even after you pay back the loan. Some investors do this, and so do students who fund their educations with loans. This can be risky, though, because the borrowing is real, but the profits may never appear.

The third cause of borrowing is impatience. We would rather pay more (including interest) to have something *now* instead of waiting a little and paying less. Impatience can be reasonable, as when a young couple borrows to furnish their new home. It is often dangerous, however, because it leads to a cycle that never ends, and simply raises our cost of living without really providing any benefit.

As you read this section on taking care of your cash flow, and as you think about borrowing that you've done or are considering, ask which of these reasons led to your debts.

HOW MUCH HOUSE IS RIGHT FOR YOU?

The biggest spending decision that most people make is where to live. It is also the easiest way for a family to get into trouble for a long time. The right decision, however, can be the cornerstone for financial success for the rest of your life. And like most decisions, it's never too late to make it better.

As a target figure to keep everything in balance, your mortgage should be no more than about twice your annual income. At this level, you'll spend about 25% of your gross income on housing. The mortgage payment will take about 18% of your income. Add in taxes, insurance, utilities, and a repair fund–figure over time on spending about 1% of the value of the house each year on major items like landscaping, roof repairs, and new appliances–and there goes one-fourth of your income. The banks and the realtors would be happy to "help" you buy much more, but (a) it may not be a good investment, (b) you may not want the rest of the lifestyle package, and (c) you have other important things to do with your money.

There are three things that are important to understand as you think about housing. **First, a house is a place to live–it is not an investment.** This hasn't always been true, but it's true more often than we like to think. Housing prices were high in the US in the 1920's, but it wasn't until the early 1950's that many homes recovered their former values. Thanks to large families, household formation, and general prosperity, we had a real estate boom in this country from the 1950's until sometime in the 1980's, when the rules changed. In places like Colorado and Texas, the real estate crash came about 1985; in California and Washington, D.C., it was about 1989.

For most of the 1990's, average home prices barely budged in many areas. According to the Wall Street Journal, prices in most major cities grew by less than 2% per year from 1990-1998, and in Los Angeles, the average price in 1998 was lower than it had been in 1990. There was a price pop at the end of the decade in many areas, but we don't know how long it will last.

Your situation may not even be that good. While the "average sales price" has gone up a little over time, the "average house" of ten years ago is now ten years older than it was, and ten years older than the competition. The roof is older, as are the dishwasher, the carpets, the air conditioner and heating and plumbing. Part of the cost of owning a house is dealing with the effects of things wearing out. Further, buying and selling houses is expensive–it costs about 10% of the value of a house to sell it (including commissions) and move somewhere else. This means it takes a 10% price increase on your old house for you merely to break even when you buy another.

In 1997 Congress repealed the capital gains tax for most real estate (except for people with very large gains). This is good news for people who had hesitated to move to smaller homes or less expensive areas because of the taxes they'd have to pay.

In the 1970's and much of the 1980's, it seemed that houses would steadily go up in value by 10% a year, so people should buy as much house as they could qualify for. You shouldn't count on that happening again. It might, but probably won't, for most people.

Second, a house is part of a package, and a lifestyle. When we choose where to live, we look beyond the house to the "community" or "neighborhood" it's part of. Will we like it there? How are the people? The schools? The shops? This is natural and appropriate. But we also have to consider the total budget impact of the decision.

The first level of spending is easy to think of, though we usually underestimate it. A new house seems to call out for new furniture. The yard needs to be landscaped, and who's going to mow the lawn? Taxes may be higher, and utilities, too. You may need a new car if your commuting pattern changes.

Once you're in the house, a second level of spending might insinuate itself into your life. We used to call it "keeping up with the Joneses." How does your car look on the street? Where do your friends shop? Where do their children attend schools, and go for vacations and camps? A house or apartment that you stretched to afford could become too much when these other items creep into your budget and lifestyle.

Third, it's OK to rent. The "American Dream" is supposed to include owning a detached house in the suburbs. There are other options, though. In a world of flat real estate prices, the cost of buying a home that you'll keep for only a few years–especially if your employer won't pick up the cost of moving–can be excessive. One of the real psychological advantages of owning your own home is that you can decorate it to fit your needs and personality. That doesn't work so well if you plan to resell the house soon, and you think you'll need to put it back into a more neutral, sellable form.

Since the cost of buying and selling a house can be high, it may make more sense to rent an extra few years than to buy something small now–say, a condo–with the hope of "moving up" with the equity you'll accumulate. Many townhouse and apartment communities are priced fairly for renters or owners, which is another way of saying real estate prices won't go up faster than rents.

SHOULD YOU PAY OFF YOUR MORTGAGE?

One of the big questions people ask financial planners is whether they should make extra payments on, or even pay off, their mortgages. If your other goals are being met and you love your house, there's nothing wrong with becoming debt free. You get a guaranteed rate of return on the money you're no longer borrowing. (Paying off an 8% debt is like earning 8% on an investment, as far as your balance sheet is concerned.) More importantly, at some point you have the flexibility to eliminate a huge item from your budget. And if you have trouble saving money, paying down the mortgage is a form of automatic savings.

However, there is a downside. The only ways to get the equity you have in your house out again are either to take out a new loan or sell the house. Both of these can take time, and require others to approve. If you need the money in a hurry, you can't get it. It's better to make sure your other savings and investing programs are in place, and that you won't ever need to spend the money "in your house," before you prepay the mortgage.

LET'S TALK ABOUT CARS

While a house is usually the biggest single purchase most people make, the money spent on cars can also have a major impact on your financial life. In most cases, cars are bad investments, and it's hard to know how much to spend. In their book *The Millionaire Next Door* (published in 1996), Thomas Stanley and William Danko reported that most people they studied who accumulated wealth never bought their cars new, and rarely bought flashy or expensive cars.

Because cars wear out and need to be replaced, there should always be a car payment in your life. If you can make that payment to yourself, not to a bank or finance company, you can either spend less or get more car.

A sound guideline is that a household with only one car should spend about 4% of its gross income on car payments, and 3% per car for a family with two cars. With a $60,000 income, 4% is $200 per month, 3% is $150 per month. At $85,000, these rise to $280 and $210; at $120,000, to $400 and $300. When you add in another 1% per year per year per car for maintenance, that gives you about 5-8% of your income for car ownership.

When you start out, that doesn't buy a lot of car. A $200 payment at 9% for 48 months allows an $8000 loan. (At 3% interest, the principal could be $9000.) Add in a $5000 trade, and you have $13,000 to spend for a car.

At the end of 48 months, don't stop your payments, just

redirect them. If you pay yourself $200 into a savings account earning 6% for three years, you'll accumulate another $8000. The next time you go shopping, you'll have a $5000 trade in, $8000 cash, and can pay cash, or buy more car. If you save $200 per month for the next seven years, you'll have $21,000 available for your next car, plus your trade-in. Your permanent budget will work well for you, once you're out of debt.

Go back to the Monopoly money. If you really want to spend more on housing or cars, you can—but you have to cut back somewhere else. By holding to these general targets—25% for housing, 5-8% for cars—you can fit more goals into your life. You'll have Enough Money.

NOW, WHAT ABOUT THOSE CREDIT CARDS?

There's an interesting way to look at the "everything else" category of your budget, all those things that are not covered under taxes, housing, cars, insurance, charity, and saving for retirement and education. Nearly everything else—food, clothing, vacations, uninsured medical expenses—can be paid for with credit cards. And many of us do just that!

Credit cards are a marvelous invention. They make our lives simpler, especially when it comes to spending money. Credit cards make it easy to conduct business, and allow us to make purchases by mail, over the phone, or through the Internet. We no longer need to carry cash or checks (in emergencies, we can rely on the cousin of the credit card, the ATM card). Stores and restaurants can process transactions faster, and with assurance they'll be paid. At the end of the month, we get a single, itemized bill that we can pay with a single check (or a few keystrokes, for the digitally connected).

That works fine, when we use it properly, but it's so easy to lose control. Unlike writing a check or counting out cash, signing a credit card receipt doesn't even require you to be aware of how much money you just spent. A trip through the mall can produce a small pile of receipts that could represent a large chunk of your income for the month.

A recent study published by the Federal Reserve Bank of St. Louis shows that most people do not have major credit card balances, but it's a big problem for those who do. Looking at Americans with average incomes, half carry no balances or have balances equal to 10% of their monthly income or less, which they could (or do) pay off. A third of the group, though, carries balances that *exceed* their entire monthly income, often by a lot. They could be in trouble.

The key to credit card usage is to keep the cards paid off every month. You get the convenience benefits without the enormous costs. If you carry any balance from one month to the next, there is no grace period. The high interest rate (usually 12 to 22% per year, or 1% to 1.8% per month) kicks in immediately. If you pay only the minimum required payment, your total interest costs for a given dinner or piece of clothing will be greater than what you spent in the first place.

Here's how to get out of credit card hell. Many people carry "permanent" balances that never seem to go up or down much. This means they're living within their budget on an ongoing basis, and need help getting rid of the old debt once and for all. It's not complicated, but it requires you to pay back the money you borrowed:

1. Determine how much is 10% of your income. That's what you're going to devote to this project. Give yourself two or three months to get up to the full 10% if you need to. Once the credit card debt is gone, this 10% can be the basis of your long-term savings program.
2. If you have more than one card with a balance, at any one time you'll be paying only the minimum on all but one of your cards. If you are putting $600 per month into the project,

and you have four cards, each with a $50 minimum, pay $50 on three cards, and $450 into the target card.
3. Make a list of all the credit cards you have, how much you owe, and what the interest rates are.
4. Find the card with the *smallest balance*. Pay it off first, regardless of the interest rate. From now on, all new purchases will be on that card, and that card absolutely must be paid off in full every month. (If you're going to face a big expense that has to be charged, like rebuilding your car's engine, put that on another card, so your "convenience" card can remain clean.) Otherwise put your other cards away, or cut them up.

(For those who cannot imagine being without a stack of cards, one great idea is to put all your extra cards in a small plastic bowl, fill it with water, put it in your freezer, and leave the cards there. That way your cards are available in an emergency, but not on a whim.

5. Once one card is paid off, next devote all extra money to the card with the *highest interest rate*. As that card is paid off, move to the next highest rate card, and so on until you have paid off all your cards.
6. If you get a chance to transfer balances to a new card with a low interest rate, that can save you some money, but don't abandon your efforts to become debt-free. Even 7% or 9% interest adds up quickly, and the low rate is quickly replaced by a high rate after a few months.

If your credit card balances equal your income, it will take about a year for this method to clean off your cards. During that time, you will stop spending 105% of your income (which is how you got into trouble) and start living on 90% of your income, and that will not be easy or fun. When you add up all the money you've been wasting on credit card interest, though, the impact will actually be less than it seems.

MANAGING THE LUMPS OF INCOME AND SPENDING

Most discussions of cash flow assume a steady rhythm, with the same amount coming in and going out each month. It would be nice if life were only that easy. But for a growing number of Americans, income is "lumpy." There may be a big annual bonus representing 10 to 50% of your total income. There may be commissions that are large one month and small the next.

Expenses, too, come in bunches. Tuitions, insurance bills, holiday presents, vacations, and car repairs often represent big checks that have to be written when the money isn't always there.

How do you deal with those irregularities without losing control of your cash flow? The answer is to build an island of calm in a sea of turbulence.

One of the favorite recommendations of financial advisors is for everyone to have an "emergency fund." If your income is variable, this concept really has to apply to you. The reason your income is variable, after all, is that whoever pays you cannot guarantee a regular payment stream. The positive side is that you can share in the benefits of extra profits or sales. If business isn't good, though, you are going to share in the pain, quickly and directly.

Therefore, you have to plan to live on less than your expected income, just in case. Figure out what you made last year and what you expect this year. Take 90% of the smaller amount, and build a budget around that. Put all of your income into a savings account (we'll deal with mechanics in a minute), and "pay yourself" a regular salary each month. Some months you'll pay yourself more than you bring in, some months less. You will gradually build up an emergency fund that can keep "paying" you if you have a bad year. This approach requires some discipline. Ask yourself how you will manage if you don't get any bonus at all this year. If you don't have a good answer, and if there's any chance of the bonus not coming through, you'd better go back to the drawing board.

One way people handle this is to live on *this year's* income and *last year's* bonus. That gives them time to adjust to unhappy news.

On the spending side, the idea is similar. (You'll see where this is going in a minute.) Add up all the predictable big expenses that come once or twice a year (tax bills, insurance premiums, and so on), add in an amount equal to the monthly surprise item (car repairs, weather damage to the house—there's usually something), and put the money in a designated account just for those purposes. This way you'll know the money will be there when needed, and you don't have to wonder what else your checking account is going to have to cover.

PUTTING THE MECHANICS IN PLACE

In a world of multiple incomes, unpredictable expenses, and long-term goals, how do you keep all this straight? Set up an extra account or two.

All your income, from all sources, should go into a master account. Paychecks should go in automatically, along with tax refunds, bonuses, big gifts, and other sources of income. From this, write one check a month for the "big ticket" items that come up once or twice a year into an account that's just used for that purpose. Write other checks to your investment and savings accounts. Write a big check to your operating account, to cover your mortgage, food, clothing, and the general expenses of regular living. The master account should never fall to zero. You have Enough Money.

RULE TWO

TAKE CARE OF YOUR INCOME BY INVESTING IN A CAREER DEVELOPMENT FUND FOR YOURSELF

Your Lifetime Balance Sheet allows you to picture your financial life in a single image, combining the Resources you have available and the Obligations you want to satisfy. In Rule 1, you learned about keeping your short-term Obligations under control so you could reach your other, longer-term goals. In this section, it's time to focus on the Resources side of the ledger.

The money you will create by working is, if you are typical, by far the biggest item in your Resources column. Except for those who are at or near retirement age, or for that small number who have all the wealth they'll need, the value of the income you have yet to earn is usually far greater than the total of investments you have built up so far. When people look for a job, they pay proper attention to the salary and benefits that come with the options they are considering. Yet many people put less thought and work into building their long-term income *potential* than they do searching out a good deal on a car or a savings account.

You want to have the flexibility to make good decisions about the work you'll do. A key tool for that–and the focus of Rule Two–is the creation of your Career Development Fund.

A LIFE OF CAREERS

Much of the discussion of work seems to start from a premise that each of us will have a single "career." We have "career counselors" in high school and college, and take tests to find what "career" we are best suited for.

This is a model that goes back hundreds, even thousands, of years, and still works for some people. Many professions provide training to people in their 20's, and offer a career track that makes later entry difficult. Most of the partners at large law firms, professors at major universities, and doctors worked their way to their current positions directly from school. Yet even here, we find many detours and lateral movements. The number of people who start in one field with one employer and stay there throughout their lives is becoming smaller each year.

Most people will not only have many jobs throughout their lives, they will also have many careers. While statistics in this area are suspect, experts commonly predict that people will have eight jobs—that is, will work for eight employers—during their lives, and that half of their job changes will be involuntary. It is common today to see twenty-somethings plan to change jobs every 12-18 months until they are 30, and even after that, plan never to work at one place for more than five years. Whether that represents the perception of this generation that they live in a world of constant change, or their inability to imagine making a commitment while so young, nevertheless, the vision of today is radically different from that of the 1950's.

It's not just employers that will change—it's what you will be doing. Entire fields are being created, eliminated, and redefined all the time. The job that you will be doing ten years from now may not have even existed when you went to school. In fact, it may not have been created yet. How can you be sure you will be competitive for it when it arrives? The companies themselves are changing, too: "Westinghouse" is now "CBS," having decided to sell its engineering and manufacturing businesses and expand its interests in broadcasting. Who knows what business AT&T or IBM are in, much less what they'll be doing in ten years? Finally, you should want to be able to change on your own initiative, not just to respond to the world around you. Your interests will change along with your abilities, and you will want to explore the opportunities that the world now offers. The amount of risk you are willing to take, or the responsibilities you want to assume, will change, often in unpredictable, or at least non-linear, ways. This can come in the form of the classic "mid-life crisis," but it often just reflects personal growth. When it happens, though, the job and path you are on may suddenly need to be changed for you to be happy.

You will also want some non-work intervals in your life, too. When a baby comes, for instance, one or both parents would often like to spend more time at home. Many times, if finances permit, one parent will stop working until their children start school, or both parents will get off the "fast track" to be there for their children. Other family events—the care of parents, for example—can also create a need to slow down at work. Sometimes, people simply want six months or a year off, to regroup or try something new.

YOU ARE REALLY SELF-EMPLOYED

A good starting point for thinking about creating the work and career path you want is to realize that you are really self-employed, and you should act like it. Self-employment simply means you alone are ultimately responsible for your career and income. Being self-employed isn't easy, but it does give you more control over your future.

The difference between being employed by somebody else and being self-employed is shown most clearly by what happens to income. Workers who get paychecks think all that money is theirs to spend. If they show up for work next week, they'll get another paycheck, and so on.

The owner of a business knows a different world. She knows that even after all the bills are paid and the payroll is met, she doesn't get to keep all the income that's left. A business owner needs to plow some money back into the business so there will be customers and income next year. A successful business is constantly working on advertising, customer research, new products and services, and other ways to expand, or perhaps just to stay even.

If you think of yourself as "You, Inc.," you can see that you need to be acting in a similar way. Suppose you are a human resource specialist for the government, or an editor at a large company. If your perspective is limited to your current job, what happens when your employer "downsizes," or "spins off" your division, or "outsources" your function? What if the next step up in your abilities would require a job that doesn't happen to be vacant in your firm, and isn't likely to become vacant for many years?

The picture changes if you consider yourself simply "under contract to" your corporate employer. If the employer changes its need for you, that doesn't change who you are or what you do, just who your next "contract" is with. If you want to upgrade your "editorial" business, maybe you will need to get a new "client." More likely, if you've taken yourself and your abilities seriously, it is likely that your current employer/contractor will want to keep you and use your new level of skills. Either way, though, you are in control.

Depending on your goals, you should plan to devote 3-10% of your income to the maintenance and growth of "You, Inc." In the long run, the amount you have left over will be much greater, and produce more satisfaction, than if you spend it all now and have no protection against the workplace changes you will encounter.

YOUR CAREER DEVELOPMENT FUND

It is easy to see what a business owner needs to reinvest for, but what is the purpose of the Career Development Fund of "You,

Inc."? Your Fund is designed to pay for many of the things you will need to enhance your income and your employment opportunities throughout your life. Such as:

—Education, formal and informal. You may know that someday you'll want to get your MBA degree. Those are expensive, and financial aid is not as readily available to adults as to "traditional" students. Even if you aren't looking for a degree, you may want courses to enhance your computer skills, learn public speaking, or master a foreign language used by your company's customers. At some point, you may want to change careers, and that often requires training in a whole new field. Having money available for that training makes the transition much easier.

—Professional associations and networking. Americans love to join groups, and there are associations for almost every business field. By joining, participating, and going to meetings, you will know where your field is heading and you will meet the people who can help you get there (or that you will want to bring along when you move). These groups, and the conventions and publications, cost money, but it is usually money well spent.

—Home computer and skill development. Ten years ago it was a good idea to have a home computer. Five years ago it was common, and today, it's essential. It's likely that someday the computer will be replaced by a new device that we will all have to acquire and learn how to use. It's usually good to be one of the first to get and learn the tools. You don't want to be the only person in your group without an e-mail address.

—Career counseling. At some point, many of us want to reevaluate the directions we chose when we started working. Sometimes the field has gotten stale or has changed a lot, sometimes we're what's changed. Maybe the kids have grown, or you've gotten excited by something new and would like to learn more. If you have the resources to pursue formal career counseling, your chances of making the right decision are enhanced. Career counseling is usually less expensive and more productive in the long run than a red convertible.

—Time off. There often comes a time when you need or want a break. It may have to do with kids or parents needing your help. It may simply be that you feel you've become stale. Some companies now provide a three to six months sabbatical with pay for some of their top people, figuring that's a better investment than losing these people altogether. What if you don't work at such a place? It would be great if you could pay your own way.

—Relocation. Sometimes we move from city to city at our employer's expense when we get transferred, but not always. What if you simply want to pack up and try somewhere else? What if your spouse gets a great chance to in a new city, but there isn't an automatic job for you in the deal. Having the money to finance a search and move gives you a lot of freedom.

—Start-up money. The number of people who literally create their own "You, Inc." each year is growing. They see an unmet need and an opportunity to do it themselves, and want to try. Unfortunately, the failure rate among new businesses is quite high, and the most common reason is lack of capital, which equates to lack of enough time to make it work. You may be there someday, and having money would help a lot.

—The "I Quit" fund. There often comes a time that the work environment becomes intolerable–pressure, harassment, dishonesty, who knows. People who don't have the resources to leave and find something else to do absorb that stress and either take it out on themselves or their family. Having the ultimate freedom to walk out the door

if things become truly awful can often give you the strength to stand up and try to fix it. And if that fails, leave.
—Financial planning and professional advice. Employment compensation packages today are increasingly complicated. It would help if you could consult a professional to be sure you are getting what you need and deserve, and you have selected the best choices for your benefits. Stock options are growing as a form of compensation, and they offer a good path to wealth if the company is successful. However, it is easy to make a mistake without help.

You will not need to spend money on all these things, but it is a good bet that at least some of them will be in your future. As a general rule, 3-5% of your income should be devoted to your Career Development Fund, and more if you anticipate going back to school for an advanced degree that you will have to pay for.

This money should be automatically taken from your paycheck and deposited in a separate account for this purpose. The investment fund should be low risk—a money market fund, or a short or intermediate term bond fund, with some perhaps in a balanced (stock and bond) fund. This is emergency money, so it needs to be safe, but some of it might not be used for a decade or more. If, at the end of the career, you haven't needed it at all, take your boss along on a nice vacation, because your work experience must have been wonderful.

USE THE BOSS'S MONEY, TOO

Many employers offer programs to pay for the items on the list we just described. Education benefits are offered in some form by over two-thirds of mid-sized and larger employers, but few employees—often only 10%—take advantage of them. The tax laws encourage employer-funded education programs. Other employers will share the cost of professional memberships, or at least grant time-off for attending meetings, and other benefits are available as well. It is one of the simplest, yet often overlooked, rules of financial planning: if someone else will pay the bill, it is usually a good idea to let them.

Be aware that some employers expect, or contract for, continued service in exchange for the benefits. For example, a computer company may send programmers for training and certification on a new program, but require that tuition be repaid if the employee leaves the company with a year. That seems fair all around.

HOW THE WORLD OF WORK IS LIKELY TO CHANGE

Having a Career Development Fund, and the attitude of self-responsibility that goes with it, will be increasingly valuable in the future. There are two main changes that will make it so.

The first is that pay for work is becoming increasingly "contingent." It is still common for many workers' pay to be fixed in advance, but the higher up you go, the more likely you are to encounter alternatives. These come in three main forms:

—Commissions
—Bonuses
—Stock options

Each of these is a step away from certainty. Each makes your pay dependent on how well you do your job and how much profit the company as a whole enjoys. Stock options in particular can be wonderful or worthless, and there is little that you personally can do to control the price of your company's stock. On the other hand, if everyone is focused on creativity, efficiency, and delivering good value, then hopefully profits will rise and with them, the value of the company. That's the idea.

What this trend means to you is that you are expected to control your "value," and you have to be able to deliver it, or expect to find a new job. Conversely, if you have good "value," and you have been networking, a company that is willing to pay you better will have an incentive to find you. Seniority and tenure alone will not assure you continued economic success.

The other change we expect is a reversal of the movement to early retirement. If you follow all the Rules in this book, you should have Enough Money to retire about "on time." As we discuss in Rule 3, though, the responsibility for saving enough has been shifted from employers to workers, and many people will not create enough wealth.

One result of this may be a steady extension of the period that people work. Retirement may stay the same length, but increased life expectancies will be tacked onto the working years, not the retirement period.

An analogy can be seen with the participation of women in the workforce. Fifty years ago, it was uncommon for married women with children to be employed on a full-time basis. This was still true, although less so, thirty years ago, but by then, their daughters were getting the same education and training as their sons. (Not quite the same, and the gender equity battles are still going on, but today it is more likely that a 20-year-old woman is in college than a 20-year-old man, and a majority of law students are women.) Today, most married women under 45–even those with young children–are working full time. Some work because they want to, others because they have to; but the system prepared for change before the change occurred.

The situation with seniors is similar, but delayed a generation. It used to be rare for a non-professional over 65 to be employed full-time. It is still uncommon, but people in their 40's and 50's are getting new training and staying in better health than their parents. As the baby boomers move into their 50's and 60's, the average age of retirement will begin to rise, and for many, "retirement" in the way the term is used now may never come.

If you have created and used your Career Development Fund through your life, you will have experienced successful job and career changes. If your circumstances require it, you will be ready to start another new career in your 50's. You will once again be ahead of your peers.

RULE THREE

TAKE CARE OF YOUR FUTURE BY SAVING FOR RETIREMENT USING "THE 700% SOLUTION®"

The first two rules help you get today's bills paid on time, and help you increase your income over time. Someday, though, you may not want to work any more. How will you pay your bills then? How will you do what you want? The concept of the Lifetime Balance Sheet reminds you that some of what you earn this year has to be set aside for the future. The big question is, how much?

Actually, that may be the second "big question." The first question is what "retirement" means to you now, and what is it likely to mean when you reach your 60's.

Retirement as something most people can look forward to is a pretty new concept. Traditionally, people worked until they died, which usually wasn't at too old an age. A combination of improved life expectancies, greater economic wealth, and regulation of business by governments and union agreements created, after World War II, the first generation to retire. Two-thirds of all the people who have ever lived to the age of 65 are alive today.

Now we have a generation who didn't start working until their 20's, who want to retire by age 60 or earlier and spend another

20-35 years in leisure. Is that likely? Is it intelligent? Is it necessary? Is it possible? This isn't the place for a full discussion of the topic, but there are several factors to consider.

a. As the physical component of "work" has steadily declined over the years, being replaced by communications, service, and intellectual elements, the ability of people to keep working after 60, 65, or even 70 is much greater.
b. The amount of education that workers have is greater than ever. Does it make sense to simply dismiss a well-educated workforce?
c. Many people have much of their lives defined or tied up in their work. Work provides definition of who we are, it provides structure for our days and years, it is the forum where we see people on a regular basis, it can provide a source of loyalty and greater identity. Many psychologists report that clients find retirement to be the greatest stress point in life, greater for many people than marriage, divorce, the death of a family member, or the birth of a child. How, then, did we all buy into the "dream" of retirement?
d. Average levels of health and energy have been improving every decade. Look at a picture of your parents (or better yet, grandparents) when they were the age you are now. Chances are, you look much younger than they did. Part of that is fashion, but part is reality–your health has probably been better, you exercise more, you eat better. If that's true today, then don't look at people your parents' age as the model of what your life will be like in 20 to 40 years. Why would you assume you'd want to retire when you still have lots of energy?
e. The generation of current retirees–people born before 1935– had a number of one-time advantages unlikely to be repeated. Many worked in careers that provided generous pension plans, and they paid relatively little into Social Security for much of their lives. (Medicare taxes only started in the

1960's.) The value of their homes and the stocks they invested in grew dramatically after 1975, when they were ready to take advantage of that environment. Today's workers are facing pension cutbacks, a flat housing market, high Social Security taxes, and a stock market that could grow much more slowly in the next twenty years than in the past twenty. The economics of retirement have changed dramatically.

The challenge with planning for retirement is that you have to take actions today to prepare for something that not only won't happen for a number of decades, but will unfold in many specific ways you cannot not foresee. Experts on aging point out that the most important issues that retirees face are not financial at all. Deciding where to live, building a network of family and friends that isn't based on work and child-rearing, coping with new levels of physical and mental abilities–all of these are big concerns, and should shape much of the planning of people in the ten or so years before the date of retirement. This book is focused on the financial issues that need to be addressed long before the age of 50, but it helps to keep the big picture in mind.

There are six main sources of income for "senior citizens." Let's look at them in turn:

1. **Social Security** is the general base that nearly all US workers can look forward to. In concept, it is a very good program in everything except its financing. Everyone belongs, your benefits travel with you when you change jobs, the benefits are paid as long as you live (and adjust for inflation), and benefits can be protected after divorce or death of the primary income earner. Few programs in the private sector offer that package.

   Social Security will be protected and preserved, with some modifications. Too many people depend on it for society to allow it simply to disappear. If you disagree and don't want to count on any Social Security benefits in your own future, then start saving an extra 10-15% of your income beyond what this chapter suggests.

2. **Traditional pensions** have formed a strong base for many current retirees, but corporate employers will try to phase them out as rapidly as possible in the next ten years. Pensions pay you a percentage of your final income based on how many years you've worked for your employer. Since your income normally goes up each year (by inflation, if nothing else), the value of your pension rises rapidly as you gain seniority—more years times a bigger number. In fact, if you work for one employer from age 30 to 65, over half your ultimate pension will be earned after you turn 55, in the last quarter of your career. Only about a quarter has been earned before you turn 50. If you change employers even every seven to ten years, you will never build up much of a pension.

The front end of the Baby Boomer generation is now over age 50. Companies, and their actuaries, will understand these numbers and their implications. They will see how expensive it will be to employ workers in their late 50's with a pension benefit, in a world that demands continuous cost-cutting. Two options will become obvious—either close down the pension plan or get rid of the employees through "early retirement" programs or other means. For the future, the company will offer a 401(k) program that's much less generous than the old pension.

(As an example of what can happen, the Supreme Court ruled in 1998 that a corporation can discontinue the retiree health benefits that its former workers thought had been promised to them. That was a pension cut in another form.)

Pensions are discussed again at the end of this chapter. For now, you should probably not count on a traditional pension plan if you are under 50 (unless you are belong to a union or are employed by a government agency). Maybe it will be there, but don't bet on it. Build your own savings program.

3. **Earned income** is a major source of income for "retirees," and will continue to become more important. This is a logical contradiction—"retirement" is supposed to mean you've stopped working—but it is a factual reality. Retirement for many people comes in two stages. "First retirement" occurs when you leave your main career and job, maybe get a pension, and then go back to work. Maybe your new job is something you've always dreamed of, like teaching or running a small store. Maybe it's something you do because you were forced out of your job a few years too early. "Final retirement" is the time when you no longer have any earned income.

Already many family units (individuals or couples) in their 60's have some earned income, and I predict that the percentage of seniors in the workforce will continue to increase in the future. In the last chapter (Rule 2), this pattern was described, and through your Career Development Fund, you can lay the groundwork to take a job if you need to, or want to, work as a senior citizen.

As you consider your own plans, the actions you take now about saving will be the most important factors determining whether your employment decisions after 60 are based on necessity or interest.

4 and 5. People do not like to think that their **children** or **welfare** may be major sources of income in their future. Today, people

in their 40's and 50's find themselves supporting their parents, and they didn't plan for it. Yet if you don't save, you may have to call on your children in the future. Other families are forced by a combination of bad economics, bad health, and bad planning to seek public assistance. About half the nursing home bills in America today are paid by Medicaid, a form of medical welfare. Few people want to plan on relying on either of these sources of support.

6. **Your savings and investments** will fill in the balance. Social Security will probably give you a floor. Maybe you'll be one of the lucky ones with a pension. Maybe you'll be in a profession you don't want to give up. But for most people, you'll have two choices: save enough money, or keep working. That's a choice you have to make *today*–you can't put it off.

The 700% Solution®

How much to save? After thinking through your options, you'd like to be in a position to live comfortably without relying on earned income some day, without calling on your children, and without much hope for a traditional pension. Is that possible? It is. This section shows how to do the math, and do the savings.

The goal of this section is to find a rule that applies as widely as possible. The time frames involved are lengthy–as much as 50 years or more, the length of time since Harry Truman was President. The number of changes to the economy, to society, to politics and daily life are likely to be as least as great as we've seen in recent decades. Therefore, we will restrict ourselves to some basic assumptions and predictions, and recognize that the best we can hope for is to learn how to point in about the right direction and move at about the right speed.

I believe that a single rule works for almost everybody. It can fit you if you have more than ten years to retirement and your income and wealth are greater than the poorest quarter of Americans (that is, if you have a positive net worth and income over $25,000 per year) but maybe not in the top 2 percent (for an age under 50, income over $200,000 *and* net worth over $750,000. A single rule: easy to understand, easy to follow, and very feasible to achieve.

The first aspect of The 700% Solution is that it doesn't measure things in terms of dollars. Even at the 1-3% inflation rate seen in the late 1990's, prices of everything grow to huge levels in fifty years. Conventional retirement projections show that a 35-year-old couple earning $75,000 per year would need over $3 million at retirement age, a number too large to be meaningful, a number so large as to be discouraging. Some of the figures used in those calculations (like rates of return) include an inflation factor, while others (like savings per month) may not. The results are very sensitive to the assumed inputs, which cannot be accurately projected.

Change your thinking, and look at everything in terms of your income. A "unit" is whatever your annual income is. Most people–probably including you–raise their spending roughly in line with increases in income. The amount of your mortgage, your contributions to your 401K plan, and your ultimate Social Security benefits are all tied to your income. If inflation picks up again, your income, and all these other numbers, will rise with it, but the ratios will be about the same.

Instead of looking at how many dollars you are saving, or how many millions you are supposed to accumulate by age 65, think of what *fraction* of your income you are saving, and what *multiple* you want to have of the income you'll be earning in the future. This way, as your personal situation changes, whether from new jobs or rising prices, your retirement goals adjust automatically.

And the math is a lot easier, as you will see.

YOUR RETIREMENT TARGET. The 700% Solution is a way to figure out how much of your income you need to save each year to be financially independent in retirement. It starts with calculating a retirement target, then determines a savings rate for you. The retirement target is the multiple of your earned income that, invested at a reasonable rate for the rest of your life, will give you the spending you need, adjusting for inflation. The process starts, then, with determining the three major inputs–spending level, life expectancy, and rate of return.

YOUR SPENDING NEED. The first step is to figure what fraction of your pre-retirement income you will be spending in retirement. You may be pleasantly surprised.

Figure your spending need on an after-tax basis. The tax treatment of retirement income is complex. Some could be from tax-free bonds or withdrawals from Roth IRAs, some will be partially-exempt Social Security, some from low-taxed capital gains, some from fully-taxed IRA withdrawals or pensions. Rather than guess what the rules will be in the future, it's better to ignore taxes and work toward net numbers.

The spending target attempts to reproduce the standard of living you had when you were (are / will be) raising children. There are several steps in the calculation:

a. The average income tax rate for most middle class workers is about 25%. This isn't the "marginal" rate, but the total of your federal and local income taxes divided by your total income. Every time Congress fiddles with the tax code, that figure doesn't change much, and it is unlikely to in the future.
b. You should save about 10% of your income for retirement. When you've retired, that can stop.
c. Most people spend 5-10% of their income on work. This can be direct, like the Career Development Fund ideas in Rule 2, or indirect, like commuting costs, nice office clothing, more

dinners out, child care, and the like. That spending is not needed in retirement.

d. You probably spend about 20% of your income on a mortgage. When you retire, you have several choices about housing. You can move to less expensive housing (either a smaller place or a different part of the country), you can have your house paid off (most seniors don't have a mortgage), or you can continue to pay. If you're going to have a mortgage, then your ultimate savings goal needs to be increased by the value of your mortgage on retirement day. You probably won't have a mortgage forever, so it's not in your budget.

e. When you have children, they are expensive, but they don't live with you forever. You can maintain your personal standard of living in retirement for less money because your children have moved out.

f. You may have to replace some lost employee benefits. You should count on spending 5% of your income on things your employer now pays for, primarily health insurance.

Here's the formula:

Total earned income	100%
Less taxes	- 25%
Less savings	- 10%
Less work costs	- 5%
Less mortgage	- 20%
Less costs for children	- 5%
Plus lost benefits	+ 5%
Net spend by and for parents	40%

When you add up all these items, *retirees should be able to live comfortably with spending about 40% of their pre-retirement gross income, plus a mortgage payment if necessary.* If all your income in retirement is fully taxable, that's about 54% on a pre-tax basis (54% less taxes = 40%). If you still have a mortgage, it could rise to 70% pre-tax on a cash basis, for the time you are in your house and paying on the loan.

The 40% figure has been questioned by many people, but it actually works as a planning target. True, if a couple has been used to spending all its income and not saving, it will take more than 40% of their income to maintain the standard of living. On the other hand, if they haven't been saving money, it is unlikely they will have the assets to support that standard of living in retirement, so they will either have to cut back or keep working and not retire. Individuals and couples who look at their own budgets and back out the amounts being spent for mortgages, children's education, retirement saving, and similar non-permanent items, find that 40% is often the amount remaining that must be replaced.

WHERE IT COMES FROM. As we noted above, retirees receive income from many sources, and this income is taxed in different ways–not at all (tax-exempt bonds or Roth IRAs), at low rates (capital gains and some Social Security), and at full rates (pensions, interests, and IRA withdrawals). This section will focus on what's left after paying taxes on the income.

The value of Social Security benefits is typically equal to about 15-20% of a middle-income retiree's pre-tax income, which equals 12% or so after paying taxes. I think this ratio will continue, or that current workers will get lots of notice before it changes.

If you need 40% of your income, and Social Security will pay 12%, then you need to replace 28% of your pre-tax income from your own investments or retirement plans to maintain your standard of living, or you'll have to keep working or accept a lower standard of living.

For example, if you earn $72,000 at the time you retire, you'll be spending about 40% of that on yourself—$28,800 per year, or $2,400 per month (plus a mortgage, perhaps). Social Security will be about $720 per month after tax (maybe more), so you will need to have $1680 per month, or $20,000 per year, in after-tax income from other sources. You might need $25,000 or $30,000 or only $21,000 in actual before-tax income, depending on its form, to get that amount. If your actual investment income during retirement is higher, some should be reinvested because, with inflation, you'll need more than $20,000 as the years go on.

YOUR LIFE EXPECTANCY. In America today, most people live past 65, but less than 5% live to 95. However, unless you expect many health problems, it's a good idea to prepare for a retirement of 35 years anyway. Health care is improving, and you might make it that long. Even if you don't, having a 35-year plan builds in a small extra margin for periods of disappointing investment returns, extra expenses, an unplanned early retirement, or one of the other surprises that somehow find everyone at one time or another. Remember, there's a 50% chance you will live longer than average. If you are relying on your own savings for most of your income, you don't want to run out of money.

INVESTMENT RETURNS. We know how much we want–28% of our income for 35 years. Now we need to know what we can expect to earn on the money we save. Here the going involves even more guesswork than we've used so far.

Over the last two hundred years, investments in stocks have generally done better than investments in bonds, and both have done better than investments in savings and bank accounts. Investments in real estate have been very unpredictable. During the 1980s and 1990s, stocks, bonds, and bank accounts did very well–the best results in American history. However, the results for the fifteen years before were much worse. What can you expect for the next half-century?

The average return on the stock market has been 6-7% more than inflation for the last fifty years and for the last two hundred years. Bonds usually produce results about three percent over inflation, and cash just matches inflation. No one should expect these returns every year, though, and the fluctuations can be dramatic. Additionally, these figures don't reflect taxes or investment management expenses (including mutual fund fees). Fees vary from 0.5% to 2% a year, and while some taxes can be deferred, they have to be paid someday.

A good investment portfolio, balanced between stocks and bonds, can be expected to beat inflation and taxes by an average of 2% per year. Over time, investment returns in stocks should match the growth of the overall economy, but owning some bonds and factoring in taxes and fees drops this a little. If 2% turns out to have been too conservative, then the "penalty" is a net worth that grows faster than expected, and you may get to spend more and save less in the future. If your expectation is 6% after taxes and inflation but you only get 2%, you will discover (too late) that you didn't save enough along the way.

CALCULATING YOUR RETIREMENT TARGET. How much money can you withdraw from an investment portfolio each year? Obviously, the more you take out, the greater are the chances you'll run out of money before you die. If your net investment returns average 2% per year, and you want the money to last for 35 years, then a financial calculator shows the beginning withdrawal rate is 4%. In other words, for every $100 you start with, you can spend $4 in the first year, $4.08 the next year, $4.20 the third year (and so on, allowing for inflation), and not run out of money for 35 years. You'll probably earn more than 4% in nominal terms, but you have to invest the excess to allow your spending to grow. If you start spending 6% instead of 4%, you risk running out of money in 20 years.

Several empirical studies have examined what actually would have happened to retirement income over different time periods.

Most of the studies support the 4% withdrawal rate as a pretty safe minimum, lasting at least 28 years even with the unluckiest timing. When the markets are favorable and returns are good, your portfolio could grow enough to allow future increases in spending, even after inflation, but bad results early in retirement cause losses that are difficult or impossible to recover from.

A 4% withdrawal rate means that you need $25 of investments for every dollar you want to spend. Earlier, we showed that you need to replace about 28% of your pre-retirement income from your own resources to maintain your standard of living. Multiplying 25 times 28% gives you 700%—**you will want to have an amount equal to 700% of your pre-retirement income in savings and investments to support yourself in retirement. This is the 700% Solution.**

What about your mortgage? This calculation doesn't include a mortgage payment, because you probably won't have a mortgage for all of your retirement years. If your retirement starts with a mortgage, then you need to have additional retirement assets equal to your mortgage balance, as part of your 700% Solution. Whether or not you pay off your mortgage early depends on your cash flow, your tax situation, and other factors, but you need to have the resources to pay it off either over time or all at once.

The first important thing to notice about the answer is that no one knows how many *dollars* you will need, because no one knows what your income will be in dollars at the time you retire, how much inflation we will have in the next several decades, or even what currency we'll be using then. (How many Germans or Italians planned for a retirement using Euros instead of Marks or Lira?) Maybe you will need $500,000, or it could be $5 million. Whatever the answer, though, if you have 700% of your income at the time of retirement, you should be OK.

Second, 700% of your income (from now on, we'll just refer to that as "700%") is not an overwhelming number. If you make

$60,000 per year now, that's $420,000 in today's money. A lot, but not impossible. At 4% inflation for 30 years, the actual dollar total could be $1.4 million, but your income then would be $200,000 per year (and an average car would cost $70,000). $1.4 million looks impossible, 700% doesn't.

Third, the calculations apply to most middle-class Americans. The target for you–700%—is the same as for your friends. The target for you today in percentage terms is likely to be the same ten years from now. Changing jobs, having another child, or other life events will not alter your target much.

The level is also self-adjusting. If you want more in the future, you'll have to save more now, unless you get a big chunk of money from selling a business or receiving an inheritance. But saving more now reduces your spending now, which reduces your needs in the future if you want to maintain your level of spending.

Finally, 700% is a good round number. It isn't precise, and that's helpful. By changing a few assumptions, the number could be 636% or 751%, but the goal is to get you pointed in the right direction, moving at about the right speed. 700% is the right direction.

HOW MUCH DO YOU NEED TO SAVE EACH YEAR FOR RETIREMENT?

Applying The 700% Solution to your financial plan doesn't require dozens of assumptions and lots of heavy math. Determining your saving rate is a three-part process–get three numbers, do one calculation, and look up your results on a chart.

The basic idea is that the money you've saved so far for retirement will continue to grow (by 2% per year more than inflation), and will represent part of your 700% Solution. You then need to save a fraction of your income each year to make up the difference.

A. You need to supply three numbers:

1. How old are you? _____

2. How much do you earn each year? _____

3. How much do you have saved for retirement? _____

This calculation assumes that you are going to retire at 65. If you want to see the impact of early retirement, adjust your age accordingly. A 40-year-old who wants to retire at 60 has 20 years of savings left, so he should consider himself as age 45 for this exercise. Married couples of different ages can start the conversation now about when they want to retire.

When figuring your earned income, remember to include any retirement plan contributions (401K) or other savings program in your gross. Your income is probably higher than your W-2 tax form report suggests. On the other hand, do not include any taxable income (like mutual fund dividends) that you reinvest and don't spend. (If stock options are a big part of your compensation, you have other financial concerns and should probably have a financial planner anyway. Don't count them as income until you cash them in, but do count them then.)

When looking at the amount you have saved, don't include money that is for goals other than retirement. The college fund and the down payment account and the savings set aside for a new car are good to have, but they don't count for this. On the other hand, make sure you include all your retirement plans at work.

B. There is one calculation. Divide your retirement savings (3, above) by your income (2, above). This gives you your starting point. If you have $120,000 in retirement savings and you earn $60,000, you are now at 2.0, or 200%.

Savings / Income : _____

C. Find yourself on the 700% Solution chart. The vertical axis is the savings you've accumulated so far (200% in the last example). The horizontal axis is your age. Find where they cross, and choose the closest curve, or estimate if you are between curves. That curve shows the savings rate that should take you to 700%. For example, if you are 40, and have saved 200%, you need to save about 11% of your income for retirement each year.

(If you're curious, here's how the calculation works. At age 40, there are 25 years for your current 200% to grow, and it should reach 328% of your future income by the time you're 65. You still, therefore, need to save 700%-328%, or 372%. If you save 11% of your income for 25 years at a 2% net return, you will accumulate an additional 348% of your future income, which is a close-enough estimate.)

Referring to the chart on the next page, your target savings rate is ____%.

Enough Money! | 83

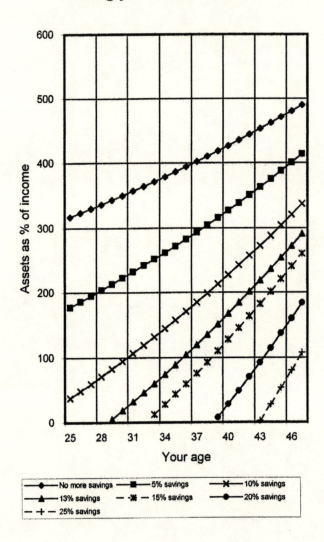

Enough Money! | 85

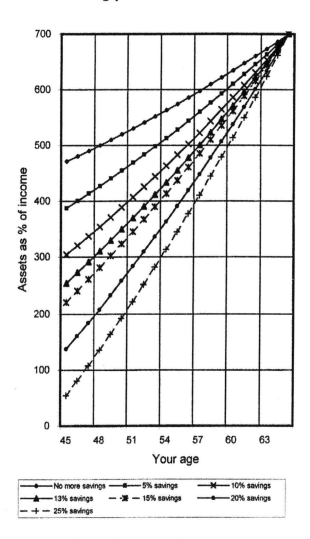

Finding your 700% Solution

When you get your answer, remember that your employer's contribution counts toward your total. In this example, if your employer puts 5% of your salary into your 401K plan on a matching basis, you only need to save 6% of your own money to reach your goal.

Only 6%! That's not pain-free, but it's probably much lower than you would have guessed possible. Looking at the table, many people will reach their goals with savings rates from 10 to 20%, including their employer's money. The fact is that long-term systematic savings and investment allows you to reach your retirement goals much more easily than anyone's ever told you before.

HOW SHOULD YOU SAVE? You've probably heard it many times, but it doesn't hurt to repeat it. **First,** whenever there is an employer match or contribution, do whatever you need to do to get it. **Second**, contribute fully to any tax-favored savings plan (like a 401K and a Roth IRA) as long as you have "target savings" available. Thus, if you can put 8% into your 401K and your target is 11%, do the 401K first, and find something else for the other 3%. **Third,** when you change jobs, be sure your old retirement savings stay intact. Either transfer them to your new plan or to an IRA. These are retirement dollars. If you need reminding of their value, look at the 700% Solution chart again. A 35-year-old who spends retirement money and drops his savings from 150% to 50% has to save an extra 5% of income for the next 30 years to make up for it. **Finally,** put most or all of your retirement plan money into stocks, but not into stock of the company you work for. Stock averages grow, but individual companies can go belly up.

WHAT IF YOU CAN'T DO IT? Suppose you are 50 and have only 200% saved so far, with no pension. The chart shows you'd need to save 25% of your income for 15 years to reach the goal. That may not be feasible for you. There are lots of ways you might have gotten into this situation—divorce, a business failure, children's education, or simply spending too much. It doesn't matter, because the past can't be changed.

If 700% is not within reach, then you will have to rely on one of the other sources of income discussed earlier in this chapter. Probably the most palatable will be remaining employed longer than you'd planned. Another choice will be a reduced cost of living. The earlier you know about it, the sooner you can plan out your alternatives. It's your life, and you do have Enough Money.

WHAT ABOUT A TRADITIONAL PENSION? Many discussions assume retirees need personal savings to supplement Social Security and a monthly pension. These pensions will be less common in the future than they've been in the past. But what if you have a job that includes a pension? Congratulations, but don't stop saving money.

Most private pensions compute benefits based on your years of service and your final pay level (or the average of your best three years), and often deduct all or part of Social Security from your benefit. If you leave a job in your forties, your final pay is usually frozen at that point, and will not be adjusted for further inflation. Your actual pension may be less than 10% of the income you're earning at the time you finally retire, and it's still subject to income taxes.

As the workforce ages, some companies, including a number of very large firms, are changing their retirement plans to discontinue or cut back on their traditional pension contributions. Other workers are given a choice of "early retirement" or reduced benefits. The plan you have may not be around in another ten years, even if you don't change jobs.

In terms of the 700% Solution, ignore a pension until you have earned vested benefits. If you are in your 30's, a pension is the equivalent of saving 3% of your income per year; in your 40's, it is worth 6% per year. Twenty years of service is worth about 250% of your income in terms of accumulation. Make the appropriate adjustments to your savings calculations.

If you are in your 50's and have been with your employer more than ten years, your employer's annual pension contribution is worth at least 10% of your income, and probably 25% of your income if you are in your late 50's with many years of service. This explains why "early retirement" offers are so attractive to employers, since pension benefits for older employees are very costly.

CONCLUSION. The numbers in this chapter are all approximate, but the amount of saving you (and your employer) need to do for your retirement is real and important. Use your employer's plans (like a 401(K) or 403(b)) fully, add a Roth IRA and general savings. The options you will have later will far outweigh the sacrifices now.

RULE THREE–A

IF YOU HAVE CHILDREN IN SCHOOL, PUT MONEY ASIDE FOR THEIR COLLEGE EDUCATION

The two biggest reasons people save money are for their own retirement and for their children's college education. The first part of Rule Three deals with retirement savings. Here, we'll look at education spending.

Unlike retirement planning, there is a huge amount of uncertainty and variation in college planning for your children. It is true that the most selective schools are very expensive–up to $35,000 per year for undergraduates in the year 2000. Two other things are also true: few students go to those schools, and few people pay full list price when they do.

Three million students graduate from high school each year, but only about 30,000 of them enroll in one of the 25 schools given the highest rankings by US News and World Report. Most students attend state or local public institutions, and many others attend schools that, although expensive, cost much less than the first tier of schools.

Further, financial aid is widely available to ease the burden of paying for college. Most schools use a common formula that attempts to calculate an expected family contribution from income and assets, and then provides a mix of grants and loans to make up the difference. At some schools, over 90% of students receive some form of aid.

In round numbers, the expected family contribution over four years is about equal to your annual income per year. If you earn $60,000 per year, you may be expected to pay $12,000 per year, or $48,000 over four years. If you earn $125,000, you may be expected to pay $38,000 per year, or $150,000 over four years. The actual formulas look at assets, family size, age of parents, and other factors. Throughout, the formulas place a much heavier weight on income than on assets, so it does pay to save for college.

As with the retirement discussion, there are many sources for college costs. Parents can pay, students can pay, financial aid may be available, loans can be taken out, work-study may be available, and lower-cost alternatively can be considered. The subject is too specialized, too complicated, and too variable from one family to the next to explore here in detail.

If you have children, start collecting information on colleges and financing when they are in grades 6-9, and work more intensively as they move through high school. You may decide that you will pay only a certain amount (such as the cost of attending a public university in your state), and your child will be responsible for the extra cost of a most expensive school. That can be a fair decision, but let your child know as early as possible so they can plan accordingly. Beware of giving your child a blank check for any expensive school they can be admitted to, unless you are sure you can honor the check without destroying your own financial plans.

If the general rule is that you will pay one year's income for your child's college, then start building up that fund early to ease the impact on your personal finances. The new Section 529 college savings plans offer many tax advantages, and are much more flexible that the prepaid college tuition plans introduced a few years ago. These accounts are offered on a state-by-state basis (and on a school-by school basis starting in 2002), and operate much like IRA plans. Contributions are made with after-tax money (though there may be a state tax deduction), assets build up tax-free, and the money comes out to the student tax-free (after 2001) and can be used at virtually any institution of higher education in the country. Grandparents can contribute to these plans as well.

The simplest rule of thumb for college saving is to subtract your child's age from 25 and divide the result into your income (up to $150,000). Once you've started saving, subtract the amount you've accumulated from your income, and make the calculation based on age.

For example, if your family income is $80,000 and you are starting a savings program for your 5-year-old, you should save $4000 this year. (25—5 = 20; $80,000 / 20 = $4000.) If your family income is $90,000 and you have $15,000 saved for your 10-year-old's school, you should save $5000. (25–10 = 15; $90,000—$15,000 = $75,000; $75,000 / 15 = $5,000.)

One thing to help you feel better is that college costs will be offset somewhat when the other costs of raising your child go away. This is obviously true if your child attends private school. The budget impact of college will only be the increase of college costs over high school costs. Even for public school students, your spending on food, orthodontia, and other expenses will go down when they leave home for college. If you have trouble saving all you should for college, recognize that the total financial impact may not be quite as serious as you had expected.

Retirement and college savings are both part of a parent's financial life, and part of the obligations of a lifetime. If you absolutely cannot do both, retirement savings should come first. Retirement plan assets are often not considered when calculating financial aid, so they are "worth" more to you. And a student can always make other choices, while the parents may not have the time to make up the retirement account. But done right, you can do both as part of your experience with Enough Money.

RULE FOUR

TAKE CARE OF THE RISKS YOU FACE BY OWNING GOOD INSURANCE ON YOUR LIFE, YOUR INCOME, YOUR MEDICAL CARE, AND YOUR PROPERTY.

We devote much of our lives to making and living out our long-range plans. We go to school, have children, plant gardens, and save for the future, with the expectation that we'll see the fruits of our efforts. Probably for our benefit, the working out of these plans is full of surprises, often pleasant ones. It's part of what makes life interesting and worthwhile.

Some of the surprises, though, bring bad news, even tragedy. Natural disasters and accidents destroy property. Diseases bring disability and early death. Fortunately, these events are uncommon enough in any one life that planning can be done to lessen the impact on ourselves and those close to us.

There are many strategies for dealing with risks. For example, everyone faces the risk of having an auto accident, but there are many options to lessen the chance an accident can ruin your life. You can:

Avoid the risk by staying home.
Reduce the risk by taking safe driving courses and driving very carefully.
Reduce the risk of injury by owning a safer car.
Reduce the size of a potential financial loss by owning an old car.
Prepare for the loss by saving money in a "repair fund."
Transfer the financial risk by purchasing automobile insurance.

In practice we may do many of these. The cost of our insurance is often raised or lowered by our driving record, the kind of car we drive, and the deductible we select. The same principles apply to other kinds of risk as well.

Insurance is an agreement in which we pay money to a company in exchange for their promise that, if some event occurs (like an accident, sickness, or death), they will write a check or pay a bill to cover the loss that results.

When thinking about insurance, remember that it is impossible to insure against everything. Some things are too rare (like a meteor hitting you) or too catastrophic (like a nuclear war) to justify an insurance policy. Some are too common (like losing an umbrella) or not important enough (like getting a cold) to make insurance cost effective. It is the items in between that give us the most concern: the events that might happen, and would have a large impact if they did. Sometimes, buying insurance is the best thing to do.

It's useful to keep this discussion in mind when you think about insurance. Remember that insurance companies, and the people who work for them, are not engaged in selfless public service. Lots of insurance is sold that no one really needs, and many kinds of insurance are really expensive for what you get. Playing on fear, guilt, and ignorance often works to sell insurance. It is commonly said in the business that insurance is sold, not bought, because it is hard to get people to spend money to face the risks that insurance protects against. While having insurance generally is good, the selling process is also subject to abuse, and the circle turns–people who are afraid of being taken advantage of often won't do even the things that make sense. So try to approach risk and insurance with some logic, and take care of yourself and your family.

LIFE INSURANCE

While more people have auto and health insurance, life insurance is what most people think of first when there is a general discussion of "insurance." Life insurance addresses one of our biggest fears–when we leave this world, will we be abandoning our families without having taken care of them? This is an emotional question. It's better to start with some facts. When are you likely to die? What would be the financial impact of your death?

A simple study addressed the first question. Over two one-month periods, once in 1996 and again in 1998, the author kept track of the obituaries published in the Washington Post, reports on a total of 703 deaths. There were only three reported deaths before age 30, and none under 18. Five percent of the stories were of people who died by age 46, 10% by age 53. One quarter of the deaths occurred at or before age 66, half after 76, and a quarter after 84.

While there are many articles about how long "everyone" is living now, only 10% of the deaths were of people 90 or older, 5% were of people over 92, and only 2% of people older than 96. Six reports (less than 1%) were of people who made it to or past age 100.

This sample is not representative of the total population–it probably overstates the economically middle class and above, and undercounts minorities, particularly Hispanics and recent Asian immigrants whose families may not read an English-language paper. You can decide if the numbers need to be adjusted for your situation.

So half the deaths were between ages 66 and 84. Very few people in their twenties, thirties, and forties die, and few people make it past the age of 90.

What happens, financially, when you die? It depends on a lot of things—are you married, do you have children, is your spouse employed (or employable), do you have other investments, is your house paid off? Think back to the Lifetime Balance Sheet. The box that represents your future income just disappeared. Five things can now happen:

—You had no dependents, so no one suffers a financial loss.
—The planned spending of your survivors will have to be cut back.
—Someone else in your family replaces your income.
—You were operating at a surplus, and the family will be OK.
—The lost income will be replaced by insurance.

While there is no universal rule of thumb, a good starting point if your income must be replaced is to have insurance plus assets equal to five times your income. The survivors receive insurance benefits tax-free, and the expenses that you had personally (your car, food, health care, clothing, etc.) will no longer be required, so five times your income is actually about the equivalent of what you would have contributed to the family over ten years. If you have substantial investments, those can substitute for insurance, and if you don't have children, your need will be less. If you have a handicapped child, or parents that you need to help, your need could be greater.

One calculation that some families use is to have enough insurance to pay off the mortgage and fund the college accounts, and then assume the surviving spouse's income will be enough to pay the other bills. If both parents make about the same amount, this may work, but there could be trouble if the surviving parent only had a small fraction of the family's income, and also now has total responsibility for raising the family.

Later in life, once you have fully retired, there may be no need for insurance, because there is no income left to replace. Whatever you are going to save has been saved. Be careful here, though, because if you have a pension that gets smaller (or disappears) when one spouse dies, the survivor may still need insurance.

One big need for insurance is after divorce. Where, in the most common situation, the ex-wife is receiving child support and, perhaps, alimony, what will happen if the ex-husband dies? The need for the income is still there, but the checks stop—a perfect case for insurance. If there isn't any insurance required in the separation agreement, the ex-wife may want to buy and pay for a policy on the ex-husband out of her own money since she is the one at risk.

Information sources like *Consumer Reports* and sites on the Internet help you estimate how much insurance you need. The calculation of an insurance agent may also be useful, but it is more likely to be too high than too low.

WHAT KIND OF LIFE INSURANCE SHOULD YOU GET?

Once you have decided how much insurance you want, the process is just beginning, because insurance comes in many styles. There are group and individual policies, term and cash value, one-year term and multi-year (level) term, traditional and variable cash value policies, even load and no-load insurance. We'll touch each of these, for they all have their place.

As an analogy, think of a couple asking where they should stay if they plan to travel to Washington or Chicago. The key is how long they plan to stay. If they'll visit for a day or a week, they should choose a hotel; if it's a year, rent an apartment; if it could be twenty years, buy a house.

Similarly, when someone asks about insurance, the first question is how long they think it will be needed. Some insurance needs are short term—assuring college funding for your high school senior or securing a large loan for a business. Other needs are long term—caring for a young family as it grows. Finally, some needs will never be outgrown—planning to pay estate taxes (see Rule 5) or taking care of the needs of a handicapped child who will never be independent. The length of the need is important because cash-value life insurance makes more sense for long-term needs, while term is more cost effective in the short run.

Term insurance is insurance for a fixed term of years, and it only pays a benefit if you die during that term. Nearly all group insurance—insurance you get through work or by belonging to an association—is term insurance. You can get one-year term, and the premium goes up every year, or you can buy five, ten, twenty, or even thirty-year term. In these policies, the price is fixed for the initial period, then usually rises a lot thereafter, maybe by a factor of ten or more. This feature assures that people are often replacing their term insurance as it gets expensive. Few companies will even issue new policies after the age of 65 or 70, and the premiums are exorbitant then. Fewer than one percent of all term insurance policies ever result in a death claim—all the rest merely expire or are dropped.

The other kind of insurance is designed in theory to last forever (or for a very long time, at least), and has a savings element in it which builds up something called "cash value." In essence, you pay too much in early years, and the extra is invested to help make the cost of insurance affordable when you get older and are more likely to die. Cash value insurance also comes in many flavors, including "whole life" (a premium is high and fixed) and "universal life" (the premium can be higher or lower depending on your expectations and needs). In regular whole life or universal life policies, the insurance company invests the money, usually in bonds, and tells you (monthly or annually) what your interest rate will be on the cash value.

It is also possible to have the cash value invested in accounts that look like mutual funds, in policies called "variable life" and "variable universal life." While the main use of life insurance is to pay benefits at death, certain tax loopholes—or, if you sell insurance, certain wise provisions of the tax code—give favorable tax treatment to cash value accumulations, and putting as much money as legally permitted into these life insurance policies can be a good way to supplement your retirement savings. Variable policies are best if you want to put a lot of money in the policy.

Cash value policies have substantial start-up expenses. As a result, it often takes ten or fifteen years for the cash buildup to be a better deal than term insurance. Thus, if your insurance need won't extend past ten years, term is probably a better idea.

When you apply for insurance, your health will be inspected. (The more insurance you want, the more tests they'll do.) If they approve you, the company is pretty sure you aren't going to die of natural causes in the next year or two. Beyond that, though, they can't be so confident. For this reason, one-year term is very inexpensive, but the premium goes up rapidly, and after three to five years, you'll probably want to replace it with a new policy. It's usually a good idea to buy a policy that has a premium fixed for as long as (or a little longer than) you think you'll need it.

Most life insurance applications are approved, and almost everyone can get insurance, though prices may vary. The best rates are offered to people who appear to be virtually immortal—great weight and blood pressure and cholesterol and all four grandparents still alive in their 90's. These are the rates you will often see advertised as come-on's, but they may be available to only 2-5% of the applicants. As testing becomes more sensitive, insurance companies can personalize the amount of risk each applicant seems to present. You may not want to know that much about your future health.

Group life insurance, to the surprise of many, is relatively expensive, especially for people in good health. This is because everyone gets coverage, regardless of their health. In most group plans, insurance rates go up as you get older, but the cost is the same for men and women, smokers and non-smokers, and people with and without health risks. Group coverage also has the disadvantage that it disappears when you change jobs, unless you want to pay really high costs to keep it. People who want more insurance than the mandatory amount provided by the group should get a personal policy if they can, instead of choosing supplemental group coverage.

HOW MUCH DOES LIFE INSURANCE COST? An insurance company should collect enough money from you during your life that, when invested, it can pay your death claim, operate the company, and make a profit. Insurance companies deal with large numbers of people, so they can assume that all people will die at their life expectancy–those who die younger will be offset by the survivors. If you are in your thirties, they have lots of time to invest your money before someone will send in a claim, so they don't need to charge much. If you start at age 55 or 60, though, they have less time, so the rates are higher. This rule doesn't quite apply to term insurance, because the company knows that few people will keep their term insurance for their whole life.

Insurance rates are determined by seven major factors: the type of insurance, your age, your sex, whether you use tobacco, any special health risks, the amount of coverage, and the agent's commission. Term insurance has a preset premium (which varies from company to company), while many cash-value policies allow you to decide your premium within a range. (The lowest possible cash value premium is rarely enough to assure that the policy will stay in force for your entire life.)

Age, sex, tobacco use, and special health risks are pretty obvious–over the next year or ten years, for example, the death rate will be higher for older people, for men, for smokers, and for people with high blood pressure or extra weight, so the costs for these people are higher. Big policies cost less per dollar of coverage to administer than small policies do, so there are often volume discounts. Finally, while agents are forbidden by law from returning (or "rebating") their commissions to customers, they often can select from several policies that pay different commissions, and there are some companies you can deal with directly, avoiding all commissions.

Insurance rates are usually quoted in cost per year per $1,000 of coverage. It is not feasible in this book to provide a table showing what different rates would be under different assumptions. Generally, though, term insurance for people under 55 is about $1 per $1000 of coverage (maybe $0.60, maybe $2), while cash value insurance is about $10 per $1000 of coverage (maybe $8, maybe $20).

Impartial information on insurance policies and insurance companies is very hard to get for consumers. In fact, while other financial products (like mutual funds) have become quite easy to learn about, the insurance industry has successfully resisted almost all efforts at disclosure. Regretfully, this obfuscation continues after you purchase a policy, and even agents often cannot get basic information on internal policy costs and structures.

HOW DO YOU BUY INSURANCE? Once you have an idea of how much insurance you want and maybe what kind, what next? For basic term insurance, it is possible to buy it from a company that deals directly with consumers, possibly over the Internet. Nearly all insurance, though, is bought through an agent. In the discussion of Rule 7, we talk about how to find an advisor you can work with in this area.

Life insurance requires a written application that includes many questions about your health. Beyond your answers, the company will probably want more information. For insurance amounts over $100,000 (or even less for older people), expect some medical tests from the insurance company's doctor or paramedical professional. In addition, the company will want information about you from your regular doctor and any specialist who has treated you for anything serious in recent years.

Most applications are issued as applied for, and over 95% of applicants are offered some coverage. Many people are afraid that a health problem makes them uninsurable, but this is rarely true. If you need insurance to protect your family, apply for it and see what happens. Should the first company turn you down or demand a higher premium, ask your agent to state your case more clearly, and to apply with other companies. If everyone comes back with bad news, pay attention—maybe this insurance is even more valuable given the risk you apparently have.

WHAT ABOUT YOUR EXISTING POLICY? This discussion so far has had the assumption that you don't have as much insurance as you need. What if that's not the case? What should you do with your existing policy?

If you have one-year term insurance that more than three years old, you should see about replacing it. If you have multi-year term that's within a year or two of running out (such as 10-year term you bought eight years ago), look to buying new insurance if you still have a need.

If you have a small old policy, you might want to keep it, but it may also make sense to use the money to help buy a new policy with lower costs or higher interest rates.

If you have a universal life policy, it is important that you check with your agent or the company about how your policy is doing. When you bought the policy, you probably received an "illustration" (a table showing how much cash value the policy would have various years in the future). Due to the collapse of interest rates since the 1980's and early 1990's, and the way some companies increased their costs, your actual cash value is probably lower, maybe much lower, than you expected. You can confirm this by looking at the cash value on your policy's annual report.

You should ask for an "in-force ledger," which is what they

call an illustration for a policy issued in the past. Ask first for a projection with your current premium and the company's current interest rates. This projection may show your policy lapsing before you expect to die, which means all the premiums would have produced neither cash values nor death benefits for you. Find out how much you should increase your payments to keep the policy in effect.

While you are learning about your policy, it's a good idea to check who you have listed as the policy's beneficiaries. You might need to change this to conform to the rest of your estate plan.

A life insurance policy is a complicated but valuable piece of property. You should understand what you have. Do not cancel it without being sure that you no longer need the policy or that a replacement is really a better deal. Even if you decide to replace your policy, keep the old one going until the new one is approved and in force.

DISABILITY INSURANCE. Disability insurance is designed to replace part of your income if you lose the ability to work due to illness or an accident. While some people may not need life insurance, nearly everyone should have disability insurance.

The purpose of this insurance is to provide you with income until you can return to work. There is a limit to how much you can buy, because the company doesn't want you to be better off by becoming disabled. Usually, the limit is about 60% to 80% of your income.

Most people get disability insurance through work. While these policies may have some exceptions and limits, they are often low cost and should be used as a base for your protection.

The tax treatment of disability insurance differs between group and individual coverage. If your employer pays the premium for your policy, any benefits you receive are taxable to you. If you pay the premiums, however, the benefits are tax-free.

Disability insurance is often harder to get than life insurance, because there are many things that can disable you without killing you—notably mental problems, stress, and back pain—and it can often be hard to determine whether an income loss is due to a disability or just a lack of business. Therefore, companies will take a close look at what you do for a living. Self-employed people working out of their homes will have a hard time getting coverage, as will those in hazardous occupations. A history of depression or substance abuse is more likely to disqualify you from disability insurance than from life insurance.

The chances of a disability are greater than the chance of dying before age 65, and the financial impact can be greater. Most people should own as much disability insurance as they can, with a benefit that lasts to age 65 or 67.

AUTO AND HOMEOWNERS INSURANCE. The world of auto and homeowners insurance, also called "property and casualty insurance," is very different from the world of life, health, and disability insurance, with different companies, different agents, and different principles.

This insurance protects your property from certain losses, and protects you from the financial impact of a lawsuit for injuries you cause. High coverage limits are not very expensive, and should usually be selected. There can be a large price difference between companies, especially for auto insurance, so it pays to check your coverage periodically. Insurance agents receive small commissions on personal policies, so they will rarely initiate a policy review for you. It's up to you.

With auto insurance, about 40% of the premiums go to pay for policy administration, including legal fees. Therefore, it is often cost effective to have a higher deductible for collision and comprehensive coverage, because the lower premiums will allow you to pay the cost of repair yourself. (An extra bonus: auto shops often charge much less if they know you are paying the bill yourself.)

Be sure to have a large amount of "uninsured motorist"

coverage, the benefit that pays you if an uninsured driver hits *you*. This is not a place to try to save money.

On homeowners insurance, full benefits are only paid if you have a policy limit of at least 80% of the replacement value of your house. Thus, if you have $150,000 coverage on a $300,000 house and suffer a $50,000 loss, you may get less than $50,000 in payments. Many policies do not automatically adjust with the change in housing prices, so your policy could become inadequate by accident. Talk with your agent or company about this.

HEALTH INSURANCE. Most people have health insurance through their work. If you have options, think about your pattern of expenses in deciding whether to pay more for a higher level plan. When you change jobs (or get divorced from an insured spouse), make sure to continue your old policy–which is now your right–until your new policy is effective. (There's a time limit for how long you can keep your old policy, so don't dawdle.)

Recent legislation has created a huge improvement in new group health insurance. For many years, people changing plans had to wait months or years for an existing health problem to be covered by the new plan. Now, if you can prove that your old plan covered it and there was no break in coverage, the new plan takes over with no waiting period. Many people couldn't afford to change jobs because of the risk of medical expenses, but now that's been fixed.

LONG-TERM CARE INSURANCE. The newest major kind of insurance helps pay the costs of long-term care, whether at your home or in a nursing home. Medicare and conventional health insurance almost never cover these costs, and Medicaid only pays if you have no other assets. It is estimated that about half of all people reaching the age of 65 will receive long term care during their lifetimes. The cost of care easily reaches the range of $40,000 to $70,000 per year. When one spouse needs care, the cost can take all the money the other spouse was planning to use to live on.

Long-term care insurance is something that most middle class people should at least investigate. If you have less than $150,000 in assets and a low income, the cost of insurance may be too high, while if you have more than $1 million in assets, you may decide you are willing to use your own money to pay the bills. The financial impact of long-term care expenses on the people in the middle could be serious, and they are the ones who will benefit most from insurance.

There are a number of good policies and companies in this field, and the details are beyond the scope of this book. Read up on it, and talk to a good agent. It's worth looking into by the time you are in your late 50's, while you are still healthy and the premiums haven't gotten too high.

RULE FIVE

TAKE CARE OF YOUR FAMILY AND OTHERS YOU CARE ABOUT BY UPDATING YOUR ESTATE DOCUMENTS AT LEAST EVERY FOUR YEARS

Estate planning, preparing for incapacity, and other inevitabilities

Imagine that, for all the money and possessions you own, you have been magically given a duplicate set, plus money equal to all the life insurance on your life. You can do whatever you want with this new money, except keep it. You have to give it away.

What would you do with it? Should there be any strings attached? Are the recipients ready for it? Should any of your gifts come with special instructions, like how to run your business or dispose of your coin collection?

Who should get the money? Would it all go to your spouse? What would happen after your spouse died? Should your children get it all? How about friends? Charities?

Now imagine that this is the *only* money you ever get to give away. When you die, all the money you have now simply disappears. The distribution you made with this magic gift was your material legacy to the world.

If you can do this exercise, you can create an estate plan.

Estate planning involves making decisions now about important parts of your life and finances against the time when you will not be able to make those decisions for yourself. Not too many years ago, estate planning mostly involved planning for death, and "making an estate plan" basically meant "having a will written."

(Think about the phrase, "last will and testament." It sums up what is happening: a clear, authoritative statement ("testament") about what you want and intend ("will"). Because you won't be around to express yourself or answer any questions, this has to be done in writing and with some formalities to make sure it's authentic.)

Recently, estate planning has taken on a second dimension. With advances in medical technology, many people spend some time before they die in a condition of incapacity, and someone else has to manage their money and affairs for them. While few people want to imagine this happening to them, planning ahead for the possibility will give you good peace of mind, and allow you to take care of yourself and your family.

There is also another dimension of estate planning—deciding what gifts you want to make while you are still alive. Many people realize they have more money than they will ever spend, and want the joy of seeing people (whether family or charities) receive it now, rather than waiting until death.

There are three stages of estate planning: the important part, the hard part, and the complicated part. The important part is deciding what is it you want to have happen. The hard part is getting yourself to do it. The complicated part you hire an attorney to do with and for you. In the next few pages we will summarize some of the rules and considerations for the important part, give you some things to think about concerning the hard part, and advise you on how to deal with the complicated part.

Keep in mind as you read this chapter that the law of "trusts and estates" is very technical and complicated. Every rule or principle has lots of exceptions and ramifications, and they vary from state to state. This section is intended to alert you to some factors you need to consider. It should not be used as legal advice. Talk to a lawyer expert in this area, who is current on the laws that apply in your state.

THE IMPORTANT PART

For most people, good estate planning is not about tax savings, because estate taxes have a reputation worse than their actual impact. In 1995, only about 44,000 estates from the entire US owed any estate taxes, about 1% of the deaths that year. Congress passed a law in 2001 that eases the estate tax and promises to repeal it in 2010, though some experts question whether Congress will allow that to happen.

When estate taxes do apply, they can be a real problem. There are five basic rules concerning estate taxes:

1. You can leave as much as you want to your spouse tax-free. Note that this rule is not much help for the surviving spouse's death.
2. You can leave as much as you want to charity tax-free.
3. If you don't own it when you die, there's no tax on it. The tax laws have ways to catch you if you play games and only partially give things away, but basically you are only subject to tax on what you haven't spent or given away during your life.
4. There is no tax on the first $675,000 left in your taxable estate in 2001, after transfers to your spouse and charity. This exemption amount rises to $1 million in 2002, with further

increases scheduled for 2004, 2006, and 2009. If you actually exceed this limit, however, the tax rate on the next dollar starts at 37%, and can rise as high as 50% under the 2001 law.
5. You don't ever have to pay an estate tax on your own money—it's always paid out of the money going to your children or other beneficiaries. This means that estate tax planning is an act of pure generosity—parents spend money or live with the terms of trusts so their children will inherit more money on a net basis. If you think your children will get enough even after taxes, there is no requirement for you to do any tax planning. The payoff to your family from a small investment by you, though, can be a hundred-fold or more.

The important reason to do estate planning for death is that it allows you to decide who should get how much of what you own, and when, and in what form, and with what strings. In starting to work on this process, begin with figuring out what you have, and where it is. Most people assume that their will takes care of everything. In terms of money and property, a will only deals with those things you own personally where other arrangements aren't already made. If you have a brokerage account that is in your name, for example, your will determines where it goes when you die.

There are two big categories of assets you might think of as yours that your will doesn't control. The first are things governed by law or by documents you have no power to change. You may own property as "joint tenants with right of survivorship." If so, at your death your joint tenant automatically owns the property, regardless of what your will might say. You might be the beneficiary of someone else's trust, and that trust might direct the property to another beneficiary at your death, regardless of your wishes. You might owe money or be subject to a divorce decree that gives others rights to your property at your death. There is nothing you can do about any of these situations by yourself.

The other group of assets not controlled by your will are items with their own beneficiary arrangements. These include:

- life insurance policies
- employee benefits
- retirement plans and IRAs
- annuities
- "payable on death" arrangements
- partnership and restricted stock agreements

Each of these should include both primary and back-up (contingency) beneficiary designations.

Thus, when you think about what you have to distribute, think about everything. When you've decided who should get how much, make sure all your documents, policies, benefits, and other items reflect your intentions.

The question of *when* beneficiaries should get money is also important, and usually applies most strongly to young children. If you have minor children, and you try to leave money to them directly, usually there will have to be a guardian appointed to handle the money. What may be worse, if the money isn't in a trust, your children will get it outright, no strings, when they turn 18. Here's a scary thought: suppose you've provided a large amount of life insurance to help your spouse raise your children, but you die together. Without good planning by you, all that money could be your children's to spend the day they turn 18.

Most people want to set up some kind of trust to hold money going to their children. That way it can be managed well, and the money can be distributed gradually as the children get older. For example, some families distribute 1/3 when the child reaches 21, half of the balance when he or she reaches 25, and whatever's left at age 30.

When you are thinking about who should receive money from you, don't limit yourself to your immediate family. A gift of a few thousand dollars could enable a family to get out of debt, or buy a new car, or send a child to college. Many charities rarely receive a special lump-sum gift that could enable them to buy a minivan or a computer. A larger bequest could endow a scholarship or rebuild a classroom (maybe with your name on it). The reduced benefit to your children from receiving $200,000 instead of $250,000 might be less than the other benefits and happiness created from what you could do with the remaining $50,000.

Also, most people leave everything to their spouse, content to wait until the spouse dies before anything goes to their children. That's the most common model, and the best one to assure security for the survivor. But if the spouse is likely to have more money than he or she can spend if they live to age 95, think about making some gifts to your children or others when the first parent dies, or even before. Your children are likely to need the money now more than they will later, after they've bought their houses and educated their children.

If you are self-employed or own a business, you need to think through what would happen at your death. Who would be the new owner(s)? Who would be in charge? What happens to your clients and customers? What about your employees? Your suppliers? Does any money become payable at your death?

These questions all appear to deal with what happens when you die, but that's not the only thing you need to think about. If you are incapacitated (from a stroke, for example, or some form of dementia), you could live for many years without the ability to manage your affairs or make decisions. It is important to set up a mechanism now so decisions can be made. Give someone (your spouse, your children, or a trusted friend) the power to step in when you can't act. Allow that person to manage your investments, pay your bills, sell real estate, make gifts, and generally take care of things. Again, if you own a business, think about how long the business should be kept going if you are not there any more. Who would be responsible? Do they know how? You should have both a Durable Power of Attorney and a Revocable Living Trust to make the lifetime management of money easier to transfer in an emergency.

THE HARD PART

The hard part of estate planning is getting it done. This requires imagining the events that have to happen–your illness or death–before the plan becomes relevant. We often can't imagine a world without us in it, or at least we don't want to. Subconsciously we may believe that we won't die if we're not "ready." We may be angry that people will get money and benefit from our pain. We may be ashamed that we haven't done a better job with our lives and people will find out. We may be so sure that our fortunes are about to change that it doesn't make sense to plan now. Planning involves unconditional love, in that we can't take these gifts back regardless of what the recipients do with them. Getting past all these psychological hurdles, and more, is so hard that most people never prepare wills.

Here are three considerations that might help you with this hard part:

1. Preparing a good estate plan is an act of great love and generosity. Most of us have had, or know about, experiences where someone died without a will or with documents that didn't work. The estate settlement process can take years if it isn't done right. The confusion and paperwork, the travel required, simply finding everything, can be a real burden. The burden often falls on your spouse or a child, who is grieving and may not be up to learning and dealing with all these issues.

Further, families can fight and even break up over money. If one child thinks you intended one thing and another child thinks something else, the argument can poison their relationship forever. A woman was told by her husband that he wanted much of his money to go to her when he died, but he never changed his will. Instead, all his money was left to his children from his prior marriage. The widow discovered she had less money that she thought, and her relationships with her step-children are strained. The clearer you can make things, the fewer fights will ensue, especially if you explain why you made the choices you did.

When you die, everyone who loved you will face grief. By setting up a clear estate plan that is easy to administer, you can at least reduce the amount of anger and frustration faced by your family.

2. Estate plans are easy to change. Your plan should be revised at least every four years. During that time, you may change jobs, get married or divorced, move, have children, have grandchildren, or acquire new assets. Each one of those changes is enough to justify a plan review, but even little things build up. The couple you had asked to take care of your children is now divorced. Your administrator moved across the country. Your bank has been merged two or three times.

   The basic framework you develop should serve you well, and the amount of legal work for many changes would be minimal. Spending a few hundred dollars every few years may eventually save your heirs from devoting thousands of dollars and many hours to straighten things out. And if you decide that you are not satisfied with the distribution plan you've created for your assets, just change it. In four more years, if you're lucky and the actuarial tables are correct, you can review it again.

3. If you don't have a will, you still have an estate plan, and you probably don't like it. Every state has procedures for "intestate" estates—estates where there was no will. For instance, if you are married and have children from a prior

marriage, your children will probably get two-thirds of your money, and your spouse one-third, regardless of need. Courts will appoint people—potentially strangers—to manage your children's money, and will choose (usually from among your relatives) who should care for them. There will be lots of extra accounting, extra fees, and extra time involved. If all your heirs can't agree on a distribution of which assets should go to whom, the court will probably simply order everything sold at an auction and converted to cash. That's the plan you leave your family if you do nothing.

So when you see the good you can create by doing some planning, and the hurt you can avoid by doing some planning, and the fact that avoiding a plan will not actually eliminate any of the events or emotions you may be concerned about, maybe the hard part of planning becomes a little less hard.

As you develop your plan, or after you finish it, talk to your family about it. The concept may be difficult emotionally, but the people who are going to be responsible for administering your estate plan (perhaps called your "executor" or "personal representative" or "trustee") need to understand what their jobs are, and where all the records are they will need. It is a lot easier to ask questions now, when you are around.

Further, if you have done anything unusual in your plans, it's a good idea to explain it to the people affected. For example, due to special needs, one of your children may get a larger or smaller share of your inheritance. There may be a charity that you want to give a substantial gift to. When everybody understands your wishes, it is more likely they'll be supportive, not angry, later on.

More importantly, the money your heirs inherit from you could be the largest lump sum they've ever had to deal with. If they handle it properly, it could change their lives for the better. If they don't know what they're doing, they could easily blow it, and have nothing left in a few years. You can help them by giving them your advice and thinking. By giving them some money while you are still alive, you can see what they do with it, and what kind of support they would benefit from.

Another major topic to talk about and plan for is health care decision making. Most people have clear ideas about how long they want to be kept alive on machines after recovery becomes impossible, but unless you write it down, you can't be sure doctors will only provide the amount of care you want. And once you've written it down (in something called a "health care power of attorney" or an "advanced medical directive", which are broader than a "living will"), be sure you discuss your plans with your spouse and children. If you've accepted the responsibility for making hard decisions, it will be much easier for others to carry them out if the time comes.

Finally, your estate plan is part of your legacy to the next generation. It represents the material part of what you want to pass on. Many of the items in it were created by your hard work, and embody some of your dreams. Don't let fear or discomfort keep you from explaining those dreams and goals to those who will follow you. Pass along the stories that go with the things, and you will add to the blessings. Further, by opening up the conversation, you may get some good feelings in return. In a more practical matter, if your children are going to inherit a large amount of money, with a high degree of probability, then that is money they don't have to save for their own retirement. They can spend more on their own children and lives today. If your children aren't going to get the windfall they might expect, though, tell them early enough so they can make other plans. The only way they can know what to expect is if they hear it from you.

THE COMPLICATED PART

The complicated part of estate planning involves all the rules of trusts, wills, and related issues. These rules are complicated, depending on who you ask, either because they were written by lawyers, or because they concern the decisions of people who won't be around to explain or correct things.

Many of the more pointless technicalities are being eliminated in most states, so the estate settlement (or "probate") process is now quicker and less expensive. Nevertheless, it is essential to work with a good lawyer, and helpful also to work with a good financial planner, as you go through this.

Choose lawyers who spend most of their time on estate planning matters. Even if your situation seems pretty simple to you, they can judge what documents you need. Thanks to automation, the cost should be reasonable for a complete set of wills, trusts, powers of attorneys, and health care directives.

A financial planner can be helpful in guiding you through the process. You can get a sense of how much of your money you'll need for your own security and whether you can start making major gifts. A planner can advise you on assets that might deserve special attention or instructions. A good planner can also help you work through some of your own emotional issues and get your plan done. Finally, a planner can read the draft documents prepared by the lawyer to see if they would actually accomplish what you want. Since your planner probably knows your situation better than your lawyer does, he or she provides a useful second set of eyes.

This book is too short to explain all the tools and techniques used by estate planning attorneys. Trusts are usually used to maintain control and management over money that you don't want distributed all at once. You can set up trusts while you are alive or through your will. Many trusts have interesting tax ramifications. One kind of trust can own your insurance policy. You can give money to another kind of trust that pays income to you for your lifetime and then gives the balance to a charity. As you add to your net worth, trusts are likely to become more useful. Some trusts can't be undone once created, while others remain in your control during your life. Ask, and make sure you understand what you're doing before you sign anything.

Your estate planning attorney is part of your team. Local estate planning councils and bar committees are good places to find good attorneys, and most planners, accountants, and insurance agents have estate attorneys they work with. If the chemistry isn't right, don't be afraid to move on. These decisions are some of the most intimate and important you will make. You need to work with somebody you respect and trust.

RULE SIX

TAKE CARE OF YOUR COMMUNITY AND YOUR SOUL BY GIVING AWAY AT LEAST TWO PERCENT OF YOUR INCOME EACH YEAR

Most financial advice is focused on building your wealth—save more, spend less, improve your rate of return, cut taxes. Here, though, it appears the advice is going in the other direction. In a sense, it is.

It is commonly assumed that people with above-average incomes would be pretty generous, because they can afford to be. In reviewing a sample of forty tax returns for clients of my firm, this was not the case. Out of the forty individuals or families, only three reported charitable gifts of more than 2% of their income, and only one gave away more than 5%. One man, unmarried, with an income of $400,000, reported gifts of only $400—perhaps coincidentally the maximum amount he could claim without having to itemize and document the gifts. The charitable message had not become part of their lives.

There are many reasons to talk about giving money away as part of your financial plan. Three seem most important:

First, it is important to keep money in its proper place in your life. Money allows you to express and experience your personal goals. Much of this book addresses the value of having a long-term perspective about money, and learning how to defer having some of the things we want now so that we'll have more security and strength in the long run. However, many people act as though accumulation and taking care of themselves are the only goals they have. That's an assumption worth challenging.

Second, we live in a community made vibrant by thousands of organizations that rely on voluntary gifts of time and effort for support. Whether their focus is on youth sports, culture, care for the disadvantaged, religion, political advocacy, historic or environmental preservation, community development, or any other cause, there are basically three ways these organizations can survive—by becoming commercial firms, by being taken over by the government, or by working as private voluntary organizations. While many areas of life now include a mixture of all three, the voluntary part is critical. All of us need to be involved.

The third reason is somewhat paradoxical. People who give money away get a greater sense of financial well-being than those who don't. If you decide to give away two or three or five percent of your income, you must have decided that you can get along OK on the rest. Of course, you would have no trouble spending lots more than you do, but doing so is not essential to your personal success or identity.

There are those who believe, and whose religions teach, that what you give away returns to you many times. This can happen in several ways, but satisfying a personal profit motive is not a good reason to make gifts. The benefits you create are much more important than that.

When you think about giving away at least two percent of your income—or at least one week's income per year—this doesn't include money given to those close to you. Buying your child a new computer is part of helping your child grow and is a good thing, but that purchase isn't included here. This rule is about giving your money to people or organizations where you have no legal or family obligation.

Not all your gifts need to go to organizations. You might want to write a check to a needy family so they can visit a sick relative in another city. You may want to help a particular child attend a summer camp. You could provide the financial help that allows a friend to adopt a baby.

Also, gifts to political candidates and organizations *are* included here. Some of the problems in American political life are caused by large donors and political action committees dominating the funding of election campaigns. When a candidate says things that make sense to you, sending him or her a check (where legal) is a good way to encourage and strengthen both the candidate and the process.

Finally, this rule does not deny the benefit of volunteering your time as a way to support others. Many efforts need time, not money—being a reading tutor to a young child comes to mind. But the rule says that the financial gifts have to be made as well.

What you support with your money and your time becomes an extension of who you are. Your values and dreams become manifest in the causes and organizations you contribute to. Because of this, give thought and pay attention to the objects of your support.

There are thousands of organizations that are doing good things and worthy of support. United Way campaigns now allow donors to designate which organizations will receive their gifts, and the lists of participating groups goes on for pages. If you have responded to direct mail appeals, your mailbox probably fills with hundreds of requests each year. You can't give to everybody you'd like to.

Focusing your support is a good way to make your money go farther and for you to have an impact that can extend beyond money alone. For example, you could decide to concentrate your giving to youth groups, groups involved with political freedom and innovation, and environmental protection. Or you could focus instead on arts and culture, health and medical research, and hunger programs, or on housing, civil rights, senior citizens, community development, and historic preservation, or on religious organizations and programs. All of those areas need help, and in the future you can shift your goals to new charities as your interests change.

The concept of focus creates extra value and power to your gifts. It allows you to develop more understanding of what "your" groups do, and you can see what your money and efforts are doing for your community or the world. If you want, you can become known to the leadership, or become an active volunteer yourself. Compare the process to growing a garden in a dry climate, when you have a limited amount of water. You'll have better results if you concentrate your water on a few plants rather than sprinkling drops over a large area.

There are several questions that can help you decide what to support. What do you care about? What are your values? Where can your gift make an impact? Where do you want to get involved? What are the opportunities for you beyond giving money? Who else is involved? Who asked you for money?

This last point is important—the most common reason people make gifts is that someone asked them. While few people like to ask for money, it's a good way to build your organization. If you think a cause is valuable enough for you to give your money to, don't be afraid to tell your friends, and give them the chance to get involved, too.

While the primary reason to give away money is altruistic, to help others, many people believe that the universe operates to provide a tangible reward to donors—what you give is returned to you many times. This can happen, and it's nice when it does.

Charitable activity can give you benefits beyond feeling good. Volunteering provides opportunities to learn or try new skills that could develop into new careers. People who give money are often invited to serve on a board or committee, and that service allows you to meet and work with others who share your beliefs and who may also provide valuable business contacts or social opportunities.

By concentrating your giving, you are likely to reach higher gift levels to some organizations, and this can have tangible benefits. For example, major donors to arts and culture groups may get first crack at tickets before the general public can buy them. If you like public recognition, major donors are usually listed in annual reports, magazines, programs, or on the institution's walls.

Through the Internal Revenue Code, Congress has created a number of rules to encourage charitable giving. The first, and most important, is that gifts to charities can be deducted from your taxable income, so part of the cost of the gift is offset by reduced taxes. Not all gifts are deductible—only gifts to charitable organizations. Generally, the group will tell you if it is a recognized charity. Gifts for the specific benefit of an identified individual are usually not deductible, and gifts to political organizations or gifts to support lobbying and advocacy are not deductible.

There are special tax provisions to encourage you to make larger gifts. If you want to make a large gift (over $1,000) and you own stock that has gone up a lot in value, you should consider giving shares of stock instead of writing a check. (The stock gift allows you to avoid ever paying the capital gains tax on the profit, and you still get to deduct the full value of the stock.) Similarly, if you have a life insurance policy you no longer need, you can give it to a charity and deduct the cash value and future premiums, with the charity receiving a large benefit when you die.

One of the best kinds of charitable gifts is one in which you give assets to a charity in exchange for an income for the rest of your life. When you die, the charity gets to keep what's left. You get a deduction now for part of the gift, you get income forever, you've reduced your estate (and estate taxes), and you've made a big gift to somebody. These arrangements go by several names, including charitable remainder trusts, charitable gift annuities, and pooled income funds.

Unfortunately, as with all tax rules, there are limits and exceptions and procedures with these special gifts. You can generally deduct gifts of up to 50% of your income in a year, or 30% if you are giving appreciated assets; any excess can be used in future years. When you want to make a gift of anything more complicated than a check, such as stock, life insurance, or a gift through a trust, talk with the charity's officials and, probably, your lawyer to understand how much you will be able to deduct and what paperwork will be required. But don't let these procedures get in the way of your generosity.

Remember charity and unexpected gifts when planning your estate. This is a good way to have your values and goals extend past your life. One man used his will to provide a lesson to the next generation about making gifts. He divided his estate into four parts. Each of his three sons was to receive a quarter. The final share was for charity, and the sons had to decide which charities would be the recipients. (Dad had a default option in case the children couldn't agree.) In this way, the sons learned that they weren't entitled to everything, they saw their father's values in action, and they had to think through making large gifts. All in all, a creative way to accomplish many goals at once.

A WORD OF CAUTION. Some people give away too much money. They contribute to every good cause that asks, or they buy cars and furniture for their grown children. They give more than they can afford, turning over income needed for their own lives and care or assets they'll need in the future.

If this describes you, your generosity could be self-destructive. It can feel good to help people who need more money, or others may try (and succeed) to make you feel guilty if you turn them down. In extreme cases, people have been known to go without medicines while they write checks for every direct mail appeal from charities they know little about.

You can give away more than 2% of your income, or even more than the 10% "tithe" amount, but be sure you are keeping enough to meet your own obligations. The recipients of your gifts are unlikely to turn around and help you if you need it someday. You may want to check with other family members to be sure your giving stays in proportion to the rest of your life.

We live in a world that we share with others, and we benefit from organizations, systems, and structures that we did not create. Each of us has a duty and an opportunity to extend that web to others living now and those to come in the future. Two percent is a minimum for that enterprise. You'll do fine, and feel better, living on what's left.

RULE SEVEN

TAKE CARE OF YOUR TIME AND YOUR SANITY BY ASKING FOR HELP WHEN THE MONEY QUESTIONS BECOME COMPLICATED OR OVERWHELMING

Everyone in our society today has to manage a number of financial decisions. One theme of this book is that the basic decisions are not too difficult, and the process is one that everyone can succeed at.

Nevertheless, there are many times when getting help and advice concerning your money is appropriate. Despite the availability of the Internet and self-help books (including this one), the path can be difficult to navigate alone. In this section we'll talk about when to get help, how to find good advisors, and how to take advice.

Decisions about money can be hard for several reasons. First, money carries lots of psychological baggage for many of us. Attitudes about money—what it's for, whether it's OK to talk about, the conflicts between spenders and savers—cloud our reason, and generate arguments in families. Many times, the process of working with an advisor can diffuse these tensions, and advisors can provide the perspective to come up with solutions acceptable to everyone.

Second, many money issues are technical and complicated. Dealing with taxes, estate planning, retirement savings, and other topics often requires familiarity with laws, rules, and options that most people don't know about and don't want to know about. Limits on IRAs, estate exemptions, education savings, and other benefits are scheduled to change annually under the 2001 tax law, making advice even more important.

Third, when we are dealing with our own money, we often lack perspective and appropriate distance. Someone else can show us options we might have overlooked, or simply remind us of other goals we may have forgotten.

Fourth, most people can develop a routine about their money, but at times of transition, this routine breaks down. The most important time for advice is when you have one chance to make a big decision. When people change jobs, get married, get divorced, retire, have children, see children leave home, lose a spouse, have stock options, or sell their company, they are likely to have new resources or new obligations that can either be handled properly or lost irrevocably. We all know the stories of people who win lotteries or receive insurance settlements, only to have all the money disappear within a year or two.

Fifth, some people want ongoing help to assure them nothing is being overlooked, or simply to provide discipline, handholding, or technical help that allows them to focus on other parts of their lives. Many folks can make decisions, but carrying them out is something they lack the ability or interest to do.

Finally, there are many benefits from having someone serve as a personal trainer or coach for this part of your life. Every top professional athlete still has a coach to be sure the athlete's skills are staying sharp and getting better. Your financial planner can keep you at the top of your financial "game" or be your partner in bringing your dreams to reality. Increasingly, planners see this function as the place where they bring the most value and change to their clients.

Each of these reasons can call for a different kind of advisor, sometimes one with technical skills, sometimes a bookkeeper, sometimes a professional consultant. When you are thinking about getting assistance, therefore, spend some time to define the nature of the problem, and the kind of help that will actually solve the problem for you. Maybe you spend too much and have trouble budgeting. Is this a technical problem that a financial planner can help you solve, or do you need help addressing how you think about money and long-term goals? People who seek the wrong kind of help can't understand why their problems persist. On the other hand, if you simply want to refinance your mortgage, for example, the questions are probably straightforward and the kind of help you need is clear.

The popular press and the people we know are eager to tell you why you should avoid getting outside advice. Many surveys show that the most common source people use for investment advice is the word of friends who probably have the same level of knowledge (or ignorance) as the person being advised. When choosing funds for our retirement account or deciding whether to buy or lease a car, we turn to people we work with for assurance and help. We have a strong do-it-yourself culture in this country. Many writers suggest that you are foolish ever to pay commissions or sales charges. We feel we ought to know this stuff, and we're afraid of looking stupid. We are afraid the advisors will be too pushy, or too expensive, or that we'll be cheated. We'd rather buy a software program or surf the Internet than talk to somebody.

A good advisor, though, will learn about your situation and know the available options, so you can understand when the choices your friends suggest aren't right for you. Good advisors are honest, and are subject to regulations that help keep them honest. The cost of good advice is not high. As someone said in a related context, if you think education is expensive, try ignorance.

Advisors come in many varieties. Some are very specialized, some are generalists. Basically, they can help you in three ways:

—They help you identify and understand the choices you have
—They help you make and carry out decisions
—They provide technical knowledge and expertise to help you navigate the minefield.

You should recognize that training and focus differs from profession to profession, and the kind of problem they expect and solutions they suggest are shaped by that training. Each has potential conflicts of interest, which sometimes are as simple as wanting to use their skills to solve your problem (perhaps so they can get paid) when another set of skills might be more appropriate. Understanding how advisors get paid (and by whom) is one key to working successfully with them.

The financial advisor with the broadest training is a Certified Financial Planner practitioner. To receive the CFP designation, a practitioner must pass a comprehensive test covering insurance, investments, retirement planning, taxes, and estate planning, *and* have three years of experience, *and* follow requirements in ethics and continuing education. As generalists, CFP practitioners may not have the detailed skills or knowledge needed for some specific situations. Most good CFP practitioners, therefore, work with other professionals, especially attorneys and accountants. With the consolidation in the profession, most organizations and respected writers recommend working with a Certified Financial Planner practitioner.

Certified Public Accountants have traditionally focused on tax and audit functions, but are increasingly moving into more general financial planning work. By their training, they often pay special attention to tax planning.

Attorneys are licensed to practice any kind of law, but you should choose an attorney who spends most of his or her time in the area you are concerned with. Relatively few lawyers are current and expert in the intricacies of advanced estate planning issues or problems in family law, so make sure yours is competent on the concerns you have. While accountants in many states are allowed to take fees and even commissions related to investment recommendations, lawyers have stayed much closer to their traditional role and independence. Few law firms offer real financial planning advice.

Psychologists (and psychiatrists, and clinical social workers) are paying more attention to the problems of money, but few of them have financial, as opposed to psychological, training in this area. If your issues seem to center around emotional or interpersonal issues that come out as money problems, working with a professional in this area could be a big help.

Bookkeepers often offer services that help you deal with your money (paying bills, keeping records, etc) on a less costly basis than accountants would.

Many financial products have specialists that focus in a single area. They can be very good with the technical concerns of that issue, but remember the adage: "When your only tool is a hammer, every problem looks like a nail." *Stockbrokers* are now often called "account managers" or "financial consultants," but their goal is to advise you on your investment portfolio. *Life insurance agents* have a professional designation–Chartered Life Underwriter–which requires passing a series of courses on insurance, retirement, taxes, and related areas. (Some also become Chartered Financial Consultants, or ChFC, which includes additional financial planning studies.) *Mortgage brokers* often work with independent companies and have access to money and programs from dozens of lenders. *Realtors* help you buy or sell a house, and can also help you own and manage real estate for investment purposes. *Private bankers* and *trust officers* can guide high net worth people to the full range of services offered by a bank.

There are two specialized sets of professionals people may need to consult at some point. If you have more debts than you can handle, there are *credit counselors* with Consumer Credit Counseling Services who help debtors negotiate a plan to deal with their debts short of bankruptcy. If you want or need to make a job change, there are *career counselors* who can help you through that process and guide you to a decision that will work for you in the long run. These people are usually independent of employment agencies, and work for you.

When you are deciding whether or not to work with an advisor, the first step is to understand what the nature is of the problem you want help with, and who is most likely to provide that help. Unless you are very clear that it is a technical concern, it is usually a good idea to start with a financial planner or other generalist.

The next step is choosing a specific advisor from the many who practice in your area. Most people start with personal recommendations, finding someone who has worked successfully with a friend or colleague. Others check with professional societies (through the phone book or the Internet) for referral programs, or call on people they've read about or seen on TV or in an advertisement. The two major financial planning organizations merged in 2000. The Institute of Certified Financial Planners and the International Association for Financial Planning joined to become the Financial Planning Association.

Once you have a candidate, you should learn about his or her background and experience (education, professional groups they belong to, continuing education, length of time in the field, special training in your area). You should confirm that they offer the services you seek, and that they work with people like you. (You probably don't want to be someone's largest or smallest case.) Find out how they are paid, and by whom. (Commissions require that you buy something, while fees may be generated by the advisor doing more or different work than you really need. In many cases, a Realtor who assists someone buying a house is paid by, and technically works for, the seller. Stockbrokers may make extra money selling new issues rather than existing stock. And so on.)

Most importantly, make sure you like and can work with your advisor. A good financial planner or estate planning attorney will ask you to discuss things you may have never spoken about with another individual. If the relationship is to work, you must have confidence in his or her judgment, honesty, integrity, confidentiality, and ability to relate to you and understand your situation. This usually takes at least one meeting to establish, and maybe several. Don't be afraid to tell an otherwise fully competent planner that you just don't think it would work out. You will be doing everyone, especially yourself, a big favor in the long run.

Don't lose your common sense at the door when you work with an advisor. There is almost never a hurry to make a decision, and feeling rushed is a good hint that you're getting bad advice. At some point, though, you have to make a decision, and a good planner encourages you to act when you are ready.

If someone suggests something that seems too good to be true, or too "close to the line" for your comfort, you should almost always say no. Either ask for additional information and other options, or get a new advisor. We want to believe that we can double our money quickly without risk and without taxes, but that almost never happens and can never be promised.

It is also important to remember that even the best advisors and organizations make mistakes. Some of these are errors of communication, when they didn't listen to you (or you to them), and something is done that you never intended. Some are errors of execution, when an account number is entered incorrectly in the computer, or the wrong security is sold, or a dividend doesn't get credited properly. These kinds of errors are usually correctable, but you share the responsibility for catching them. Look at your statements and reports and tax forms, and ask questions if you see something that doesn't seem right. A good advisor will be able to fix most things and make you whole.

Errors of judgment or prediction are something else. Most financial decisions involve some degree of assumption about the future. Unfortunately, companies fail or disappoint, tax laws change, countries change governments, and other things happen that were hard or impossible to forecast. A good advisor will let you know the range of things that can happen following a decision, and those are often risks you must take.

A poor advisor may cover up or be unaware of risks, or otherwise recommend inappropriate actions to you. Advisors cannot eliminate the risk-return tradeoff, and they can't control or change the world for you. If you feel you've been poorly served or taken advantage of, talk to someone else you trust for a second opinion. You have many options, from talking with your advisor to moving to a different advisor to taking action against your advisor. Don't simply allow yourself to feel like a helpless victim. You aren't.

When you think about working with advisors, it's useful to recognize the three zones of responsibility along the spectrum of decision making. The spectrum runs from those things that only you can decide, to those items you share, to the things that involve implementation that you don't want to (or can't) be concerned with. For example, the decision whether to save for retirement is one that you have to make, while the decision of who is going to administer your company's 401(k) program is something you can't do anything about (unless you happen to work in the human resources department). Here's a picture to help you see how this works.

WHOSE DECISION IS IT? YOURS OR YOUR ADVISOR'S?

Zone One	Zone Two	Zone Three
Basic goal questions	Action policy ideas	Technical details
Your decisions	Shared decisions	Delegated decisions

All the decisions in the first zone are yours. They are the kind of things dealt with in the Seven Rules—are you going to pay your bills? Take care of your family? Plan for your career? Give money away? These are basic decisions that nobody can make for you. Good conversation and probing questions from an advisor can help you frame your goals and values, but they should be *your* goals, not your advisor's.

The third zone deals with the details of your financial life. For instance, mutual fund companies will reinvest your dividends for you automatically if you choose that option. How that happens is not something you should worry about.

The area in the middle includes topics where you and an advisor work together and share responsibility. You have made a basic decision ("I want to save for retirement"), but you want help deciding how much you need to save, what plan to choose, and which investments to own. The advisor brings you choices, and you select a path to follow. (The actions that implement the decisions fall in the final zone.)

You have total control over where the lines are between these three zones. You could decide that everything is in Zone One. For instance, if you prepare your own tax returns, you may not have anything for anyone else to do with your taxes. On the other hand, you could delegate almost total control of your investments to a manager, at which point you have minimized the first two areas, and maximized Zone Three.

You have to take responsibility for wherever you place the lines. Many people like to avoid the basic (Zone One) decisions because they are hard and have long-term consequences. They would prefer to parachute directly into the details (Zone Three) and spend time redesigning an investment report format or monitoring their investments on an hourly basis. It is common, and unfortunate, to see people micromanage their investments without ever defining investment policy or goals. It is easy to be lost if you never decide where you want to go.

Financial success is most likely when you spend your time in the areas where you are responsible and getting advice to help make good decisions. If you want to implement your decisions, go ahead. For the best use of your time and energy, you may want to allow professionals to do most of the heavy lifting and detail work that carries out your wishes.

THE NON-RULE ON

INVESTING

HOW YOU INVEST YOUR MONEY MATTERS, BUT NOT AS MUCH AS FOLLOWING THE SEVEN RULES DOES

Financial planning and investment management are not the same thing. Financial planning is taking care of all the aspects of your financial life so the money you have is sufficient to support all the things you need to do. Investing is (or should be) what you do after you've followed the other rules. It is the decision of where to put the money you've generated through the good decisions you have made.

This is not the way most people seem to look at investing. Federal and state governments, for example, regulate financial planners through laws dealing with "registered investment advisors." This is somewhat justified, as many financial planners are redefining themselves as "wealth managers" or "investment management consultants." Many of the specific questions planners are asked in public presentations deal with investing, and clients often define whether they need financial planning advice by the amount of money they have available to invest. In many ways, the investment decision seems to drive the process, often to the exclusion of other important issues.

Investment decisions do matter, and good investment policy can improve your long-term results. This section deals with how investments work, what kinds of expectations you should have, what you should pay attention to, and how you can invest intelligently.

However, good investing isn't required for success, and good investing can't save you from bad decisions elsewhere. At a recent workshop, a young employee asked how she should invest the money in her retirement savings account. It turned out that she was contributing only 1% of her income to the plan, and as a result, was losing out on most of her employer's 5% match as well. It doesn't matter much what she invests in, because even the best option will not give her the results she needs. Instead, she was advised to set aside at least 5% of her income so she'd get the full match, and 10% (plus the 5% match) would be better. Yes, a stock fund would probably do better for her than the guaranteed option, but adding 10-15% of her income to the plan each year is more important than how she invests the small amount she was contributing.

A couple in their 60's illustrates the opposite point. The husband was an executive in the non-profit world, and had set up a deferred compensation program with his employer in 1980. (This is a plan in which some of his income was set aside to allow him to get payments from the plan when he retires, to supplement his other retirement programs.) In 1980, the stock market had been doing poorly for over a decade, and interest rates were over 12%, so the advisor setting up the plan recommended that his money be invested in the most conservative option, a money market fund. He stayed with the employer for eight years, and let the money build after that, but he never changed the investment option. At his next job there was a similar plan, and he again chose the "safe" option. Now he's ready to retire, having almost totally missed out on the greatest bull market in stocks in

American history. But guess what? By following the rules, the man and his wife will still have a very comfortable retirement income—much less than they might have had, to be sure, but still quite adequate.

This couple raised and educated three children, and they certainly could have used the extra money along the way instead of setting it aside. If they had, though, their situation today would not have been as good, and they are satisfied with the overall balance they have achieved.

This couple's strategy also illustrates the choices we make among the various goals of investing. When people invest, it is first to *preserve* capital, then to *grow* capital, and finally to *spend* capital or income. After a long period of good times, people often forget the first goal. Yet Will Rogers notably said, "I am more concerned about the return *of* my capital than the return *on* my capital." We forget that markets go down as well as up, and we forget that if we lose enough, we might never recover. Real losses are possible, painful, and have real consequences. When the couple in our example thought about retirement, they wanted to be sure that they did not lose the money they'd set aside, and getting a little interest on it so it kept pace with inflation was sufficient for them.

They had enough time that they could have done better, but their personal or family memories of the Depression and financial setbacks may have made security a very important goal to them. Without learning how to balance those memories against the way investing usually works over long periods, the conservative option probably felt good to them. More education might have let them do something else with at least part of the money.

The primary point of this "non-rule" is that you understand how your long-term results and success are controlled and determined. There are three factors:

The first factor is the *return on the investments* you own. This is not the most important, and is one you can't control very much.

Your return on (or of) your money is determined mostly by how you allocate your investments among the kinds of things you can own (stock, bonds, etc.), and much less by the timing of moves in and out of the market or the selection of specific stocks, bonds, or funds.

The second determinant of how much money you'll have in the long run is *investment "leakage."* This you can control more. Most people underestimate how much they can lose through fees and expenses in the investment process. Selling one stock and buying another usually costs between 2 and 4% of the amount invested, between commissions and investment spreads. Discount brokers and on-line trading are less expensive than traditional brokers, but the costs are still substantial. Mutual funds and money managers cost between 0.3% and 3% per year, and they have transaction costs in addition to that. Good advice, as we explained in Rule Seven, costs money and is often worth it, but careless investing can be expensive.

Taxes are another part of leakage. Using tax-deferred investments, owning tax-free bonds, and holding onto investments to get preferential capital gains tax treatment are all ways to reduce the tax bite. Taxes can eat up a third or more of the returns on some investment strategies.

The final, and most important, determinant of your results is *your behavior.* This is highly controllable by you. You need to resist two temptations—the temptation to spend the money too soon (money you should save or have already saved), and the temptation to give in to restlessness, fear, or greed by playing with your investments too much. There are few short-term strategies that work, so turn off *CNBC*, put down the *Wall Street Journal*, and don't trade stocks from your cell phone or Palm Pilot. Keep your mind on the long-term goals you're building for.

Let's look at investing, and address some of the more traditional issues. What are the basic kinds of things, or asset classes, you can invest in? The most common way to split up the categories is between stocks, bonds, cash, real estate, and other assets. Each of those classes, though, includes a wide range of different things with their own levels of risk and potential return. There are high-risk bonds and low-risk stocks. There is a better way to think about your choices, dividing them into five groups:

LOW-RISK ASSETS—These are investments where the primary goal is to preserve the dollar value of the investment, and perhaps to give you a little interest income, too. Typical low-risk investments include checking accounts, certificates of deposit, money market funds, annuities, and whole (or universal) life insurance cash values. The value of your defined benefit pension can be included here as well. When people talk about "savings" as opposed to "investments," they are usually thinking about this category. One thing to remember here is that what you protect with a low-risk investment is the number of dollars, but not necessarily the purchasing power of that money. Also, many "Low-Risk" investments are not guaranteed by the government, so you may still face some risk of loss. All these descriptions are relative.

In every category, you can either invest directly in assets of the type described (stocks, bonds, savings accounts, etc.), or you can own mutual funds that give you a diversified selection of securities in the category.

INCOME ASSETS—Here the return is mostly from regular interest earnings, while the principal itself may be fluctuating somewhat. The returns are usually larger than from Low-Risk investments, but there is some risk of price changes and even default. Most Income investments are bonds, which can include US government issues, corporate bonds, tax-free bonds issued by local governments, and bonds issued by foreign governments and companies.

GROWTH ASSETS—Growth investments may have some return from income (like dividends), but mostly, you hope the value (price) of the investment increases. The typical Growth investments are stocks (or stock mutual funds), including stock from companies either large or small, American or foreign based. A diversified portfolio of leveraged real estate (property with mortgages) or real estate investment trusts would also be a Growth investment. Despite the hopeful name, Growth investments don't always grow in value.

BALANCED ASSETS–Some investments provide returns from both income and price changes, while others invest in a wide variety of assets types. These Balanced investments typically provide returns and risks between the Income and Growth categories, though they can have special risks of their own. Many people like Balanced mutual funds (often with 60% stocks, 30% bonds, and 10% cash). Other Balanced assets include high-yield (or "junk") bonds, and rental real estate on which there is no mortgage, producing current income.

VENTURE OR AGGRESSIVE ASSETS–These are investments where it is difficult to predict what kind of return to expect. Results may depend on lots of borrowing, or on one company's performance, or the price of natural resources. Examples include stock options, new stock issues or private investments, raw land held for development, or the value of a company you own and operate. Other types of Aggressive investments would include highly-leveraged real estate, precious metals, and investments in developing markets or emerging industries.

Sometimes the investment technique can transform regular assets into Aggressive assets. "Day trading"–investing for extremely short periods from your home computer, often with borrowed money–is extremely risky, even if the underlying stocks and bonds are not. The Aggressive category would also include almost any investment that represents more than 20% of your net worth, because a sudden price change could have a big impact on your overall wealth.

"Savers" tend to focus on Low-Risk and Income investments. "Investors" focus on Income, Balanced, and Growth, depending on their temperaments and objectives. "Speculators" spend their time in the Venture/Aggressive area. Few people (other than people with their own businesses) end up with much lasting profit in the Venture/Aggressive area, unless you count the recreational value of the excitement involved. There is something called the "90-90-90 Rule" that applies to people who engage in day trading of stocks, options, and futures: 90% of the people seem to lose 90% of their money within 90 days.

One of the most important developments in investing in recent years has been the rediscovery of the concept of not putting all your eggs in one basket. The idea is now called Modern Portfolio Theory, and it says, briefly, that different investments work together better than you might think. Imagine two investments that change in value independently–say, a piece of real estate and a stock. Each of those might be fairly risky to own, with a 30% chance of losing money. But if you own *both* of them, you might only have a 10% chance that both will lose money, and only a 20% chance that your total portfolio will go down (for example, that the stock will go down more than the real estate will go up). By adding another risky asset (the stock) to your initial risky asset (the real estate), you've cut the overall risk you face! The men who figured this out won the Nobel Prize.

What this can mean is that you can have a relatively conservative portfolio in two ways. You can invest only in "low-risk" things, or you can invest in a lot of *different* things. In fact, you can sometimes reduce your risk level by adding new investments with higher, but different, chances of losing money.

There are two practical problems with Modern Portfolio Theory. One is that moving from the intuitive, general discussion we have just had to a detailed application requires the ability to predict the level of risk, the expected return, and the degree of independence (called "correlation") of every asset class you want to consider. Nobody can predict any of those things accurately.

The second problem is that assets are becoming less independent and more correlated. The theory works best when assets don't change in value together, but in today's world, more and more things seem to be linked. The financial problems that first surfaced in Thailand in the summer of 1997 were still reverberating around the world years later. There are differences between countries and markets and asset classes, but the world's stock and bond markets move together much more than they used to.

These are technical problems in applying the theory, but the basic idea is solid. Your broadest choice is a globally diversified portfolio that includes stocks and bonds from different countries plus real estate, cash, and sometimes other investments as well. Designing this matrix is more of an art than a science, but the objective is to seek a good return without huge fluctuations from one year to the next.

What kind of investment returns can you expect? That is a harder question than it appears at first blush. The most common type of investment advising is based on predicting investment returns, but that approach asks the wrong question. Follow along.

First, for most investments, when we ask what the return has been for a certain time period (like a year), we are combining the "Economic Return" and the "Valuation Return." The Economic Return is how the company (or bond, or piece of real estate) did—how much income or interest did it generate. The Valuation Return measures the change in how much "the market" is willing to pay for that economic return.

Economic Return tends not to change very fast. A company has the same number of employees, customers, and products from one month to the next; a bond pays the same interest amount every six months. Yet when a stock is being bought, it is not so much for the current profits as for the future profits, and expectations can change very quickly.

The Valuation Return can be specific to a company, so that what seemed attractive on Wednesday suddenly is not attractive on Thursday. Every week there are stocks that change in value by 30 to 50% based on some news about earnings, even though nothing major appears to have changed in the business.

Valuation Returns can also change dramatically for an entire market. The amount of money people were willing to pay for an average American company and given level of profits (the Valuation Return) quintupled from 1982 to 2000, growing at a rate of 10% per year. In that same period, the amount of money those companies earned (the Economic Return) grew by a factor of three, or 7% per year. Combining those two, the price level of the US stock market increased fourteen times (from a Dow Jones Industrial Average of 777 in August 1982 to a level of 10,800 in November, 2000). Not counting dividends, that was a price increase of 16% per year.

However, when you think about buying stocks (or any other investment), you are buying an asset at the price it has now reached. You don't get any of its historical gain. The future returns to you will depend on the combination of the future Economic Return and the future Valuation Return. If the Economic Return continues at 7% per year, the only way you can receive more than 7% is if the Valuation Return continues to grow and people are willing to pay more and more for the same amount of income. The price of earnings, now at an all-time high, would have to continue to rise and double and redouble again. How likely is that?

Suppose, instead, that the amount people *pay* for Economic Return (which reached 33 times income in 1999) drops to the average paid over the last 70 years (about 15 times income) during the next ten years. Then, even if the Economic Return grew by 7% a year, the Valuation Return would shrink by 7.3% a year, and the total return would be about zero. (Prices could drop, offset by dividends being paid.)

Economic Return is more reliable as a basis for future returns, while Valuation Return can change dramatically in a short time, either for a single investment or an entire market. Over the very long run, Valuation Return is probably zero, and Economic Return is what you will receive.

When we look at bonds, we also see a difference between Economic Returns and Valuation Returns. A bond is a promise to pay a certain amount of interest every year, plus a return of principal at maturity. When the general level of interest rates goes down, the value of existing bonds with their income stream goes up. (When new bonds pay 5%, an existing bond paying 8% becomes worth more than its face value.) Rates dropped from the 10-15% range in the early 1980's down to about 5% in early 2001, and the owners of bonds have received both interest payments and price appreciation. However, rates would have to fall to or below zero to generate similar returns for the next fifteen years. That's impossible, so Valuation Returns have to be smaller in the future.

It would be nice if it were possible to predict valuation changes, because that is where the big profit opportunities seem to be. There are two ways that it would appear possible to do that—look forward or look back. Unfortunately, neither works.

Every January and July, the *Wall Street Journal* publishes a survey in which about fifty leading economists (from banks, universities, consulting firms, and investment companies) offer their forecasts for the next six and twelve months. They predict six major economic numbers: the interest rate on US Treasury Bills, the rate on long-term government bonds, the inflation rate, the growth rate of the economy, the exchange rate between the US Dollar and the Japanese Yen, and the US unemployment rate. The article is usually headlined something like "Economists see slowing ahead." It should say, "Why do these people still have jobs?"

Since 1990, with only one exception, the actual results every time for at least one of the numbers has been outside the *range* of predictions of at least 95% (and often all) of the "experts." In one period, no one predicted the economy would be as strong as it was, in another no one foresaw the rise (or in another period, the collapse) of the Yen, and so on. For the first half of 1999, more than 90% of the predictions underestimated the growth of the economy, the fall in unemployment, and the rise in short and long term interest rates. The results for the second half of the year were similarly off for the gross domestic product, short-term interest rates, and the value of the Yen. Notice that we are not just saying the *consensus* was wrong, but rather that almost *everybody* missed major economic events that arrived within the next six months.

If you had hired these people and relied upon their advice, you would have missed every important movement in the American economy during the 1990's. You would not have been alone, of course. No one knows how to accurately forecast the future of the economy or of financial markets.

Since looking forward doesn't seem to work, what about the other way to predict valuation changes—betting that past changes will continue, or at least hiring people who seem to be able to do that through their prior investment success. The *Wall Street Journal* asked six top investors in 1992 to choose just one mutual fund each that they would buy and hold for ten years. In 1998 it reviewed the results so far: not one of the funds had done better than the overall US stock market, and several had done even worse than the average fund in their class.

Bigger picture forecasting has an equally dismal record. In 1980 and 81, we had a general consensus about the future in the American economy. Oil prices would reach $100 per barrel by 1990, we would face high inflation for a long time, real estate and hard assets would do well, but owning stocks would be a mistake. Every part of that forecast was wrong. Oil prices didn't exceed $28 until early 2000. Inflation has mostly disappeared, house prices did not rise for ten years, gold is one-third of its former price, but stocks have risen fifteen-fold.

In the late 1980's, we were told that "Japan, Inc." would soon take over the world; eleven years later Japan was mired in a depression, with stock prices less than one-third their former highs. In the mid-1990's, experts were excited about the Asian miracle, with cooperative, centrally-guided "free" economies producing growth and investment returns forever; in this case, "forever" lasted about two years. You have to wonder what are the things we are equally certain of today that will turn out to be totally wrong tomorrow.

If neither extending trends nor predicting the future can be counted on to work, then it will be unwise to base your investment decisions or expectations on those predictions.

Can't we at least rely on the "law of averages" and "reversion to the mean" to estimate future results? Unfortunately, no. While many people quote the fact that stocks (actually just the stocks of successful large US companies) have returned about 10 to 11% per year since the 1920's, few distinguish the Economic Return from the Valuation Return, or notice how variable returns have been. While we accept that returns vary from year to year, we're surprised by how much they vary over longer periods as well.

You may feel eight years should be long enough to see an "average" return, but results over eight-year periods vary widely. For the large company stocks represented by the Dow Jones Industrial Average, total annual returns (including dividends) over eight-year periods have ranged from lows of –3.71% per year (1930-37) and +0.83% (1967-74) to highs of 20.55% (1949-1956), 20.54% (1982-89), and 20.23% (1992-99). Eight-year returns for bonds since 1969 have similarly varied between 2.65% per year (1974-81) and 17.13% (1982-89). Even over 20-year periods—an investment lifetime for many people—the return on the Dow has ranged widely. It averaged 13.56% per year from 1940-59, then only 5.23% from 1960-79, then back to 18.20% from 1980-99.

Note that these returns represent averages, and do not include any taxes or fees. Individual investors would have received different, and usually lower, returns. Future results in these areas may be similar to those shown, or could be better or worse.

If stocks or bonds generally are rising in value, most diversified portfolios will also grow, while slow or declining markets will be reflected in most individual portfolios. The financial tide may be your friend or your enemy, but you can't control or predict it.

While there is a lot of uncertainty here, notice one piece of good news. Only twice in all the examples shown (stocks beginning in 1929 and 1930) did an eight-year investment end up losing money. Patient diversified investors are usually rewarded. Notice also that the average returns for stocks are usually better than for bonds, but not always.

The message is simple, if unwelcome. The returns your investments receive will matter in the long run, but they out of your control. If you can't control it, don't worry about it.

Based on this discussion, what should you think when you turn to the basic investment categories? We live in a free-market, capitalist society, and it will probably be worthwhile in the long run to be an owner of profitable assets—stocks and real estate. However, owning income and balanced assets provides real returns as well, and the outsized returns of the last ten or fifteen years will probably not be repeated.

One leading writer on investment policy, Roger Gibson, CFP, of Pittsburgh, thinks that investment decisions are based on the answers to two questions: do you think that it is possible to use skill to forecast market changes, and do you think it is possible to use skill to pick better securities than other investors can? If you think the answer to the first question is yes, you should engage in market timing; if not, pick a strategy and stick with it. If you think the answer to the second question is yes, hire a good manager (or do the picking yourself); if not, invest in index funds or a broad range of securities and relax. A third question is whether it is possible to select which markets or asset classes will do relatively better than others. If yes, pick them; if not, use a globally-diversified mix of investments.

Most people want the answer to all three questions to be "yes," since investing feels like a puzzle that ought to have a solution. Researchers have concluded that the answer to all three questions is generally "no." Using skill doesn't help, mainly because there are so many people with equal (or better) skill (or bigger computers) in the game. One alternative is to put most of your money on the "no" answers, but devote a little effort and money to finding people who might prove you wrong.

There is real value in choosing a policy–any policy–and sticking with it through thick and thin. When fashions and attitudes change without warning, the person who happens to be in the right place is a winner, after being a loser during a previous part of the cycle. Those who chase the public mood never catch up with it. Stay in one place and let the world come back to you.

This "non-rule" started with the idea that your non-investing behavior is the biggest key to the results you have. Even so, you have to make investment decisions. What kind of investing behavior should you adopt? I believe the place to start is creating an Investment Policy Statement for yourself.

An Investment Policy Statement sets out how you are going to make investment decisions in the future. The biggest threat to your investing success is that you will allow yourself to make emotion-based decisions, responding to news events, market price changes, or hot tips with greed or fear. The goal is to help yourself resist those temptations.

Your statement can be fairly simple. Define your goal, decide how much time you have before you need the money, and what money you have (or will add) for the account. Then list anything you won't do (perhaps investing in tobacco or gambling companies, or using borrowed money) and how strong your nerves are (how much of a short-term loss you are willing to withstand before you would bail out of your strategy). Next, define how you think the investing world works–do you want to try to time markets or pick securities, how much do you want to do yourself and what will you hire a manager for, will you look at the whole portfolio or each separate asset when judging results.

From this base, set a basic allocation or policy–how much will be in stocks, bonds, real estate, cash, and other things–and perhaps a specific policy–how much of the stocks will be large companies rather than small companies, and so on. Then define how you intend to select managers (including mutual funds), and how you plan to keep score. The outline of an Investment Policy Statement is in the Appendix.

Once you have an Investment Policy in place, there should be little reason to change it, or the investments you own. If the market drops a lot or goes up like a rocket, you'll be tempted to sell or buy more. Before you do, ask yourself if your objectives have changed (probably not) or if the world now works differently than you thought it did last month (also, probably not). If that's the case, then your Policy should still be valid, and you can clench your teeth and wait for the weather to change in your favor.

An Investment Policy Statement is an important step. There are some others. First, be prepared both financially and psychologically for bad news and bad results. A "worst-case scenario" is rarely pessimistic enough. (Did anyone predict that an entire major market segment, emerging market stocks, could lose over two-thirds its value in less than 18 months as happened in 1997-98? How many people expected Internet stocks to lose $1 trillion of market value in a single day in April, 2000, or that the entire NASDAQ index would drop by 60% in twelve months?) Don't invest money in things that fluctuate in price if you'll need to spend the money in less than two years. (Some people say five, or even eight, years!)

Next, control your decisions, but don't try to control results. You can't. Don't count on beating the averages, because you probably won't. One year in three, you'll probably lose money in your stock investments.

Watch out for gimmicks. The financial and investing world is littered with ideas and strategies and schemes that made a lot of logical sense, but turned out not to work. No one can guarantee you impossible rates of return. (Actually, that's not true. Many people can promise them, they just won't *deliver* them.) No one can forever repeal the link between risk and return, a fact that even the "big boys" relearn to their regret every few years.

Finally, once you've made your basic decisions, hire good managers, and leave your portfolio alone.

This path suggests putting together a group of managers or mutual funds to produce a diversified portfolio. There's an even easier path to portfolios with a good chance of success.

As mentioned earlier in this section, there are a number of Balanced mutual funds that invest in a mixture of stocks, bonds, and cash. Some of them change their allocations based on where they see opportunities, while others keep the mix pretty steady. Some will do very well or very poorly for a year or two, probably because they made a big prediction and were either lucky or unlucky with the results. Often the best fund one year is at the bottom next year. You probably don't want that one.

Here is how to proceed. There are about two dozen Balanced (or hybrid, or asset allocation) funds with over $2 billion in assets. Eliminate funds that had the best or worst results over the last one or five years, and those you can only get through a specific firm (unless you already do business with that firm). Invest equal amounts in any three that are left. If you are younger or willing to accept more risk, choose three with a higher percentage of their money in stocks. If you are more cautious and have never invested in anything but bank accounts before, choose three with low amounts of stocks. You can get a list of the largest Balanced funds from your local library, through the Wall Street Journal, or from several on-line sources. It's possible to design a portfolio that fits you better and will probably give you a better return, but this approach will get you a good part of the way home.

Once you've bought some stocks or mutual funds, keep good records. (Due to the complexity of the tax laws, the safest course is to never throw away an investment statement as long as you own anything listed on it.)

Keep adding to your portfolios from the money you're saving for your Career Development Fund and your 700% Solution goal. You'll be happy that you've committed to a path that will take you to your financial goals.

CONCLUSION

YOUR ONE-PAGE FINANCIAL PLAN AND THE SEVEN PROMISES

This book started with two ideas: everybody has Enough Money, and the basic rules for prosperous living must be simple enough to understand and follow. The Lifetime Balance Sheet provided a way to see your financial present and future in one picture that helps you understand the long-term implications of your financial decisions.

Now that you have cycled through the Seven Rules several times, you can put everything back together. Let's start with a pictorial budget, to track how your income can be used to carry out the Seven Rules.

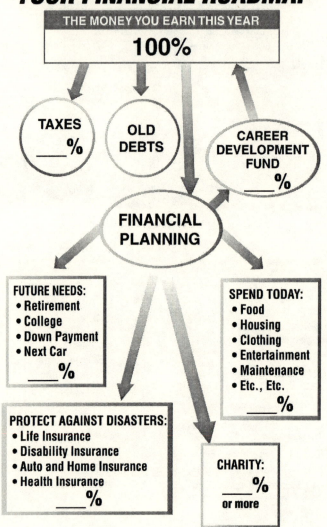

We've provided two financial roadmaps to guide you through the process. In the first, we've included typical percentages that will go for each category of spending or saving. The second roadmap lets you fill in the numbers that fit your specific situation.

Out of all the money you earn this year, about 25% will go for income taxes. Depending on your prior habits, you may need to devote another 5% to 10% to paying off existing consumer debts and credit card balances. (Rule One)

The balance goes into the circle marked Financial Planning. Peel off 3% to 5% for your Career Development Fund. (Rule Two) That money will provide the seeds that grow your income in the future. Next, add 5-15% to your retirement fund, on your way to The 700% Solution. (Rule Three) Don't forget that your employer's contributions are included in this total, so you might not have to fill in the entire amount with your money. If you are saving for college education or another major purchase, this needs to be done here as well.

Next, plan to spend 5-10% of your income on insurance programs. (Rule Four) This amount will vary a lot from person to person and family to family, depending on whether you have good benefits provided by an employer for life, health, and disability protection, and whether your needs for coverage are large or small.

Next, plan to devote 1-2% of your income to professional advice in the areas of estate and financial planning (Rules Five and Seven), and at least 2% of your income to gifts and charity. (Rule Six) Some of the money for advice might be paid from your investments, so it would have less impact on your cash flow (but it's still an expense).

This leaves you with about half your gross income to spend on the things you want and need today—food, housing, clothing, entertainment, and everything else. This is the category that is endlessly elastic, that can expand to consume as much money as is available for it. It is the category that everything else ultimately supports. By not wasting money on credit card interest, you'll have more money to live on. By increasing your income, you'll have more in the long run. By saving for retirement and owning insurance, you and your family will have what you and they will need when you've stopped working, can't work, or are gone.

THE ONE-PAGE FINANCIAL PLAN

YOUR SEVEN PROMISES FOR PROSPEROUS LIVING

A financial plan is a commitment to yourself that you'll do what you need to, so you can have a prosperous life. When you first encountered the Seven Rules, they were on one page. Let's return to that concept, but change the Rules into your Seven Promises. Your One-Page Financial Plan sets out your Seven Promises, using your numbers and your situation. As you work through these items, fill in your answers in the spaces provided. We have included two versions of the Plan, one for individuals and one for couples, at the end of this section.

PROMISE ONE–CASH FLOW. If your credit cards are all current, put "NOW" in the blank. If you have a balance, use the following formula:

> Determine 10% of your monthly take-home pay, divide that into your balance, multiply by 1.2, and that's how many months it should take to pay off your cards. Find out when that is, and

put the date in the blank. Example: If your take-home pay is $5000, 10% is $500. Your credit card balance is $3000. $3000 / $500 is 6, x 1.2 is about 7, so it will take about seven months to pay off your cards. If it's now October, seven months from now will be next May.

PROMISE TWO–INCOME. Your Career Development Fund number can be 3-5% of your income. If you have lots of employer-provided opportunities and you doubt you'll ever change fields of employment, you can use the lower end of the scale. If you have to do it all yourself or might change careers, you'll need more. If you expect to need advanced education (like an MBA), 5% may not be enough.

PROMISE THREE—RETIREMENT. In the section on Rule Three, you saw a simple formula and chart to determine what percentage of your income you need to be saving for retirement. After finding that percentage, subtract the amount your employer is putting aside. The difference is up to you. Convert the percentage into dollars, and put the amount in the blank.

PROMISE THREE–A–COLLEGE PLANNING. If you expect to pay for college education for your child or children, determine what you would expect to pay each year in today's money (after subtracting expected financial aid and the child's share), multiply by four, and subtract the amount you have saved so far. Divide that by the number of years until the child's college graduation year, and that's the amount you should be saving each year. If your children are already in junior high or high school, and you don't have much saved yet, add up to seven extra years, and plan to borrow and repay a part of the college costs.

PROMISE FOUR–INSURANCE. For life insurance, start with a figure of five times your income, and adjust. You'll need less if you have a spouse with a good income, no children, a small mortgage, or substantial investments and pensions. You could need more if you have few assets and many children. That's the amount you should have, though some of it may be provided by your employer. If you are single with no dependents, you may not need any life insurance.

For disability insurance, the base figure is usually 60% of income. Using the same factors as with life insurance, you may want more.

For auto and home insurance, you should review your policy with a good company or agent.

For health insurance, most people use what they get through work. If you don't have that option, talk with a good agent and review what's available.

PROMISE FIVE–ESTATE PLANNING. If your estate planning documents are more than four years old, put a date here of 90 days from today. Otherwise, use a date four years after you last updated or reviewed the plan.

PROMISE SIX–GIFTING. Calculate 2% of your income. If you feel motivated and generous, calculate more than 2% of your income. Put the number in the blank.

PROMISE SEVEN–GETTING ADVICE. If you have a financial planner or other advisor, list his or her name here. Recognize that you'll have other professionals on your team as well, including your estate attorney, perhaps a tax preparer, and others as needed. If you don't have a name to write down, perhaps you should get one.

THE NON RULE–INVESTING. Creating and following an Investment Policy Statement, bringing your various investments and plans into harmony, is a key to reaching your accumulation goals, once you are living your Seven Promises. Give yourself 90 days to write out a policy (though it will only take an evening or two), and another 90 days to move things around properly.

OUR SEVEN PROMISES

FOR PROSPEROUS LIVING

PROMISE ONE: We will take care of our cash flow by having all our credit cards paid off by _____, and we will keep them current every month.

PROMISE TWO: We will take care of our future income by investing $_____ per year in our Career Development Fund.

PROMISE THREE: We will take care of our retirement by investing $_____ per year, to reach The 700% Solution.

PROMISE THREE–A: We will prepare for our child(ren)'s education by saving $_____ this year.

PROMISE FOUR: We will take care of the risks we face by owning $_____ of life insurance on our lives, $_____ per month of disability insurance, proper auto, homeowners, and liability insurance, and adequate health insurance.

PROMISE FIVE: We will take care of our family and heirs by updating our estate documents and plan by _____, and every four years after that.

PROMISE SIX: We will take care of our community and our soul by giving away at least $_____ each year.

PROMISE SEVEN: We will take care of our time and our sanity by getting help when financial questions become complicated or hard to face. Our primary financial advisor is _____.

THE NON-RULE: We will follow a long-term investment strategy, and will have an Investment Policy Statement prepared by _____. We will refer to it at least once a year.

SIGNED: _____

DATE: _____

MY SEVEN PROMISES FOR

PROSPEROUS LIVING

PROMISE ONE: I will take care of my cash flow by having all my credit cards paid off by _____, and I will keep them current every month.

PROMISE TWO: I will take care of my future income by investing $_____ per year in my Career Development Fund.

PROMISE THREE: I will take care of my retirement by investing $_____ per year, to reach The 700% Solution.

PROMISE THREE–A: I will prepare for my child(ren)'s education by saving $_____ this year.

PROMISE FOUR: I will take care of the risks I face by owning $_____ of life insurance on my life, $_____ per month of disability insurance, proper auto, homeowners, and liability insurance, and adequate health insurance.

PROMISE FIVE: I will take care of my family and heirs by updating my estate documents and plan by _____, and every four years after that.

PROMISE SIX: I will take care of my community and my soul by giving away at least $_____ each year.

PROMISE SEVEN: I will take care of my time and my sanity by getting help when financial questions become complicated or hard to face. My primary financial advisor is _____.

THE NON-RULE: I will follow a long-term investment strategy, and will have an Investment Policy Statement prepared by _____. I will refer to it at least once a year.

SIGNED: _____

DATE: _____

After you have completed your One-Page Financial Plan, return to the second Roadmap. Fill it in with your numbers. Use it and your plan to structure your financial life. By combining your Seven Promises for Prosperous Living and your financial roadmap, you have a clear and straightforward strategy.

Keep a copy of your One-Page Financial Plan where you can see it and refer to it frequently. Reward yourself for making a plan, and congratulate yourself for making the plan the guide for your financial life.

It won't always be easy to juggle and fit in all your obligations. But it can be done, and your sense of satisfaction at your success will be great, knowing that you indeed have, and will always have, *Enough Money!*

THE END

APPENDIX

YOUR INVESTMENT POLICY STATEMENT

On the following pages, you will find the outline for an Investment Policy Statement, as used in the author's financial planning practice. The sections that can make up your personal statement are shown, along with some ideas for what to include in each section.

SAMPLE INVESTMENT POLICY STATEMENT OF

_____

PREFACE:

We are creating an Investment Policy Statement to guide our present and future investment decisions. We recognize that the biggest threat to long-term investment success is the force of short-term events and emotions. Therefore, we want to set down our goals, plans, and resources now, so that we have a benchmark to use in making decisions and evaluating progress both now and in the future.

INFORMATION ABOUT THE PORTFOLIO

1. THE PURPOSE OF THIS PORTFOLIO:

[Outline here what the money is for, and how long before it will be needed. Example: This represents most of what we plan to use for living expenses in retirement beginning in fifteen years. Example: We want to create enough money to pay for four years of a top level college education for both of our children, who will graduate from high school in 2005 and 2008.]

2. WHAT IS, AND WILL BE, IN THIS PORTFOLIO:

[If this portfolio represents only part of your total investments, describe which accounts are to be included. You may have more than one Investment Policy Statement. Also describe your plans to add to this portfolio. Example: Our retirement fund includes our retirement plans at work, our IRAs, and the money in Mrs. Client's name. We plan to add about $20,000 per year to our employee plans, and save another $20,000 per year for retirement.]

3. INVESTMENT CONSTRAINTS:

[Include here any "rules" you want followed. These could include your unwillingness to sell a particular stock, or your desire to invest only in companies or funds that meet tests of "social responsibility." If you are willing to consider any investment or strategy that may be suitable to your situation and objectives, you should say so.]

4. SHORT-TERM RISK TOLERANCE:

[Uncertainty and the risk of losing money, either short-term or long-term, are included in any investment strategy and every investment decision. Reducing the amount of expected risk usually also reduces the expected long-term return of the portfolio and the chance your goals will be met. Thus, a "risk-averse" strategy may have the unintended effect of increasing the risk that matters: the risk that not enough money will be there when you need it. However, while that sounds fine in theory, you still have to endure many ups and downs, some of them potentially extended, and that can be hard.

[How willing you are to experience a loss before you would insist on a change of investment strategy. When considering risk, will you evaluate each investment on its own, or will you look at the performance of the overall portfolio. Upside risk is also an issue: will you be willing to hold to a portfolio strategy when one area of the portfolio has outrun the other parts by a wide margin?

5. HOW THE INVESTMENT WORLD WORKS:

In order to create a strategy, it is important that we are clear with our understanding of how the investment world works. There are several principles that we agree with:

a. We will not rely on predictions of market results, because we do not believe anyone can accurately and consistently predict the direction of stock prices, interest rates, or other market variables over periods of less than a few years.

b. While it may be possible to choose specific stocks or funds that will outperform market averages, it is difficult, and most of the return from a portfolio will track the average (or index) of securities of a particular type.
c. The biggest determinant of how our portfolio will do is the asset allocation—the mix of general asset types, and of subtypes within each group.
d. Since markets are not predictable, it is rarely necessary or appropriate to readjust the investment allocation because of market events. The main reason to change the allocation would be a change in our situation.
e. Investment returns are highly variable, even over periods as long as a decade or two, and are largely out of our control. Therefore, it is not useful to rely on target rates of return in making planning decisions or evaluating results.
f. Despite the unpredictable nature of results, we do expect that, over time, stock ownership will probably give better returns than bond ownership, which in turn will be better than cash ownership. Variability, however, will also probably be higher with stocks than with bonds, and both have more risk than cash.
g. Different asset classes and different markets often change independently. Therefore, a portfolio that includes a mixture of asset classes, including some that would be risky on their own, can produce a good return with moderate risk. We are willing to consider the risk of an investment "in context" with other parts of our portfolio.
h. There are some managers who have historically ranged across multiple asset classes with flexibility and success, or who have a unique investment approach that has consistently worked. We would like to consider placing up to 25% of our money with such managers, even though it may not be fully consistent with our basic allocation.

2. DELEGATION

[How much investment management do you want to do on your own, and how much are you willing to delegate? At a minimum, give your advisor a clear statement of goals–this Investment Policy Statement–and insist that your advisor comply with all requirements to provide you with statements, prospectuses, and similar information and the education to understand them. Beyond these policies, do you want to be presented with a single set of recommendations, or do you want to see options for each decision? Do you prefer individual stock holdings managed for you, do you prefer mutual funds, or do you care?]

3. TAX AND LEGAL CONSTRAINTS

[Include here any special tax or legal restrictions on this portfolio. Your advisor should understand the basic rules for retirement plan accounts, but make sure they know about anything that might not readily appear. Example: This is a trust that we cannot use the principal from for 20 years. Example: This is an inherited IRA, and we are required to take annual distributions every year.]

4. OTHER INFORMATION

[Is there anything else about this portfolio your advisor should know about, or that you want to define more clearly?]

PORTFOLIO STRATEGY AND MANAGEMENT

Based on the information in this Statement, we approve the following investment policy for this portfolio:

1. BASIC ALLOCATION

The portfolio should be managed to achieve the following

balance of asset classes within a reasonable time. We recognize that market changes and the additional or removal of money can change the specific balance at any particular time, and we also know that it may take time to reach this target balance.

    Stocks _____%
    Bonds _____%
    Cash _____%
    Real Estate _____%
    Futures, metals, etc _____%

2. DETAILED ALLOCATION CONSIDERATIONS

   a. International diversification is appropriate. About _____% of stocks, and up to _____% of bonds, should be in companies or issuers outside the US.
   b. Diversification by issuer and type is appropriate. Stocks should include a mix of large and small companies, with up to _____% in stocks of small or mid-sized firms. Up to _____% of foreign stocks and bonds may come from emerging countries.
   c. Diversification by manager is appropriate. Asset classes representing over 15% of our assets should include at least two managers or mutual funds.
   d. Diversification by style is appropriate, but with a bias toward value stocks (lower price-earnings ratio, etc.), as compared to growth stocks.

3. HIRING MANAGERS

   We will select money managers as the primary tool to purchase investments in each asset class, rather than trying to select individual securities on our own. The managers may work through the mechanism of mutual funds, annuity or insurance separate accounts, or they may manage separate accounts for us.

4. MONITORING PERFORMANCE

We recognize that our goals are long-term, and short-term market results are unpredictable. While we want regular reviews of our investment situation, we will focus on how we are progressing toward our goals, how our managers are performing compared to their peer groups, and whether anything requires a change in our investment policy. Some investment styles come in and out of favor, and we recognize the need for patience. However, if a manager is consistently failing to meet the goals set for that part of the portfolio, or if a change in personnel or policy by a manager makes holding a position no longer appropriate, we expect to be informed and advised what alternative actions we should consider.

We recognize that our behavior is an important part of our ultimate success, and that our willingness (or not) to add investment funds and to hold to long-term decisions will largely determine whether we meet our goals.

5. REBALANCING ASSETS

Our portfolio should be brought back into alignment with our basic allocation on an annual basis, although small variations are inevitable and acceptable. As much as possible, rebalancing will come through deciding how new money should be invested (or where portfolio withdrawals should be taken from), rather than selling and buying assets within the portfolio.

_____
(signed)

_____
(Date)

ENOUGH MONEY !

By Richard E. Vodra, CFP

Finally, a book about money that's short and comprehensive, believable, workable and readable, that helps you

- build your income
- know how much to save for retirement
- create an intelligent investment plan
- protect your family
- control your cash flow
- know when and how to choose advisors
- see the big picture of your financial life.

The rules about money fit on one page. Read how they work for you.

ORDER FORM

Please send _____ copies of Enough Money! to:

Name: _____

Address: _____

City, State, Zip: _____

Phone: _____

Email: _____

Enclose a check for $20 for each book, plus $5 shipping and handling. (Sorry, we cannot accept credit cards, and books must be prepaid.)

Thank you for your order. Mail it to:

Richard E. Vodra, CFP
6827 Montivideo Sq. Ct.
Falls Church, VA 22043

703-538-4888
revodra@aol.com